SPECIAL MESSAGE TO READERS

THE ULVERSCROFT FOUNDATION
(registered UK charity number 264873)
was established in 1972 to provide funds for
research, diagnosis and treatment of eye diseases.
Examples of major projects funded by
the Ulverscroft Foundation are:-

- The Children's Eye Unit at Moorfields Eye Hospital, London
- The Ulverscroft Children's Eye Unit at Great Ormond Street Hospital for Sick Children
- Funding research into eye diseases and treatment at the Department of Ophthalmology, University of Leicester
- The Ulverscroft Vision Research Group, Institute of Child Health
- Twin operating theatres at the Western Ophthalmic Hospital, London
- The Chair of Ophthalmology at the Royal Australian College of Ophthalmologists

You can help further the work of the Foundation
by making a donation or leaving a legacy.
Every contribution is gratefully received. If you
would like to help support the Foundation or
require further information, please contact:

THE ULVERSCROFT FOUNDATION
The Green, Bradgate Road, Anstey
Leicester LE7 7FU, England
Tel: (0116) 236 4325

website: www.foundation.ulverscroft.com

LATTE OR CAPPUCCINO?

Red wine or gin-and-tonic? Baguette or wrap? Every day we are faced with hundreds of lifestyle choices that impact on our health. These dilemmas might seem small, but choosing the healthier option can make a big difference to your overall wellbeing. Award-winning Health writer Hilly Janes examines these daily decisions — from what to eat for breakfast to how to deal with a heavy workload — and advises which is the healthier option to choose. No longer will you dither over your dinner menu or wonder whether to walk or cycle. This clever book takes the hassle out of good living and the stress out of the small stuff.

HILLY JANES

---◆---

LATTE OR CAPPUCCINO?

125 DECISIONS THAT WILL CHANGE YOUR LIFE

Complete and Unabridged

ULVERSCROFT
Leicester

First published in Great Britain in 2012 by
Michael O'Mara Books Limited
London

First Large Print Edition
published 2013
by arrangement with
Michael O'Mara Books Limited
London

The moral right of the author has been asserted

The information contained in this book is correct to the best of the author and publisher's knowledge and contains the latest research at the time of publication. It is *not* an alternative to seeking personalized medical advice. The information contained is aimed at healthy adults. Pregnant women, children, the elderly, and people who may have different requirements should seek alternative medical advice.

A catalogue record for this book is available from the British Library.

ISBN 978–1–4448–1715–7

Published by
F. A. Thorpe (Publishing)
Anstey, Leicestershire

Set by Words & Graphics Ltd.
Anstey, Leicestershire
Printed and bound in Great Britain by
T. J. International Ltd., Padstow, Cornwall

This book is printed on acid-free paper

Contents

Introduction

If you are very slim, get lots of exercise, sleep like a log, feel totally on top of your daily schedule and never shout at your children or partner, give this book to a lesser mortal now.

If, on the other hand, you consider yourself to be a reasonably healthy adult, but you would like to lose a little bit of weight, or you sometimes feel overloaded and anxious about how much you have to do, or worry that your relationships with family, friends or colleagues are not as happy as you'd like them to be, this is the book for you.

It's here to help make simple the everyday decisions we often face. The book is based on sound medical research, advice from the most reliable experts, common sense and my own personal experience as someone who has worked for thirty years — many of them full-time — while looking after my family. And as a writer and editor on quality newspapers and magazines specializing in lifestyle, parenting and health I've been lucky enough to work with leading experts in the field. This book aims to share the top-to-toe knowledge I have built up over that time, from what neuroscience is telling us about how our brains work to why flat shoes aren't necessarily good for our feet.

The book's easy-to-digest format runs through over 120 choices that can have an impact on our health and wellbeing from first thing in the morning to last thing at night. Shower or bath? Do a piece of work or delegate to a colleague? Go for a run or a swim? Wine or gin and tonic? Pizza or pasta? Argue with your partner or bite your tongue?

But we are drowning in healthy-living advice already, I hear you say. We are indeed bombarded regularly with advice from health professionals, the food, drink and fitness industries, relationship gurus and so on, but the advice seems to change from one minute to the next. That's partly because medical research evolves all the time, and while no one would want to be prescribed drugs or undergo medical procedures that have not been rigorously tested, the words 'studies show' can raise a lot of questions: who paid for the study — a drug-company with vested interests? How and from whom was the data collected? Did the published results include any negative findings? Are media reports accurate? A September 2012 review in the journal PLOS claimed half are subject to spin. So it's with these questions in mind that

I've tried to find the most solid sources (listed in full on pages 196–99) to back up the choices in this book.

One of my aims is to demystify the confusing messages sent out to us by the food and drink industry. Labels like 'healthy' or 'natural' sound as if they are good for us, but actually mean very little. Food companies and supermarkets want us to eat and drink more — tasty food that's often full of cheap, processed ingredients can mean big profits for them. Similarly, the catering trade offers us bigger and bigger portion sizes, often for little extra cost. The trouble is the more primitive, hunter-gatherer parts of our brains find these extra portions hard to resist. Combined with our increasingly sedentary lifestyles, it's no wonder 60 per cent of us are now overweight. Poor diet is raising our risk of heart disease, diabetes and some cancers, but this can be reduced, or even reversed, by changing how we eat, drink and exercise.

The good news is that this book is full of examples of how to make these changes with little food and drink swaps that can make a big difference to calorie intake, as well as fat, sugar and salt levels — food groups that can really tip the balance towards ill health if we don't keep an eye on how much we are eating. Some simply presented facts and figures about nutrition at the end of this book on page 187 are designed to help you understand the basics. There are tips, too, on how to improve the amount or type of exercise you get and stay motivated, even if your idea of participating in sport means jumping up and down in front of the TV.

You may be in terrific shape, but perhaps you need some help with relationships, or psychological problems. Some psychologists, psychotherapists or counsellors and most complementary therapies are not regulated by law, however, so their advice may not be backed up by proper qualifications or codes of conduct, and you take it at your peril. So, I have turned to trustworthy sources, such as academics who conduct sound research and professional associations with rigorous standards, to underpin my advice.

Think of this book as a sort of recipe book — it's been designed to allow you to dip in and out of it with ease, picking the topics you like the sound of and that you know will work for you. Perhaps you already make some of the choices suggested in this book. Nobody would expect you to follow it slavishly, but I hope that if you do take up some of the suggestions, you'll find some ingredients for a happier, healthier life.

First Thing

A bad start in the morning can leave you feeling grumpy and anxious well into the day. Think: you can't find the right clothes, you've run out of milk and a child's lost its homework — well, the stress mounts. A simple routine will set you up for whatever lies ahead.

Freshening Up

The decisions you make in your morning bathroom routine will perhaps be dictated by time constraints, with you or other members of the family queuing up to use the facilities. The good news is that most of the decisions you have to make here are pretty quick and time saving.

Shower OR bath?

Have you ever wondered why Scandinavians swear by taking a hot sauna, followed by a dip in freezing cold water? It's because it's thought to aid circulation — the heat brings the blood to the surface of the body and the cold drives it back to its core. Why not try jumping in the shower and adjusting the temperature of the water to help your circulation? It also has the added benefit of boosting the blood flow to your brain because your head is exposed to jets of water, and directing the hot water at stiff or painful muscles also acts as a type of massage.

Both a five-to-ten-minute bath or shower will add moisture to the skin, but any longer in the water may leave it less hydrated than it was before you started, according to the American Academy of Dermatology. To counteract the effects of a long soak in the bath or shower, the Academy recommends using a soap or body wash that contains moisturizer, and rubbing a moisturizing cream or lotion into still-damp skin when you've dried off.

Taking a shower, lifestyle gurus say, uses less water — a precious resource as the world population grows and developing countries' demand increases. As personal hygiene accounts for about a third of water requirements in the UK, it makes sense to use as little as possible — but, as the UK's Department of Environment, Food and Rural Affairs (DEFRA) points out, a shower typically uses around nine litres a minute, and if we stand under it for more than ten, we might use more water than we would in a bath (which, depending on the size of your bath, uses about eighty litres). Keen greens can surf the Internet for shower timers and collapsible buckets to collect waste water for the garden or to wash the dog, in order to keep shower time as efficient as possible. Not such good news for lovers of a long, relaxing

soak in the bath, so if that really is your preference see Last Thing on page 144 for tips on how to get the most out of one.
ANSWER: shower

Did you know?

. . . that the average water use in England is around 150 litres per person per day? That's like 317 pints of milk on your doorstep. It is consistently higher than the average amount of water used in European countries such as Germany and Holland. In Germany, for example, average use per person per day is 127 litres.

Short- OR long-term hair removal?

There are so many ways of dealing with hairy legs, armpits and bikini lines, all with various pros and cons, that it's hard to say which is right or wrong. For the short-term solution razors are quick and convenient for legs and underarms, but you probably wouldn't want to use them on your bikini line or face. Shaving can also cause irritation, cuts and even infection if the razor is not kept clean. Shave in the direction of the hair growth, and make sure your skin is moist. Consider using a shaving oil (the type men use on their faces); apply body lotion afterwards to keep your skin soft and smooth.

As for supposed longer-term solutions, creams are messier and take longer to use but are a better option for smaller, sensitive areas. They work by dissolving the hair, turning it into a jelly-like substance that can easily be wiped away, and they contain moisturizers to soothe and soften the skin. While the chemicals they contain can be smelly, the industry has got better at masking this with fragrances and also developing different products such as roll-ons, sprays, and varieties that can be used in the shower. Regrowth is softer but not slower than it is with shaving, and creams may cause irritation or allergic reactions: always test on a small patch of skin. They are messier, more time-consuming and more expensive to use than a razor.

Waxing is good because it pulls the hair out from the root — ouch. For the faint-hearted, salon visits are the obvious option, but they are expensive, time-consuming and, of course, not something you would do every day. The same can be said of electrolysis and laser hair removal.

ANSWER: shave (where appropriate)

Did you know?

. . . that using a razor to shave your legs and arm-pits does not make the hair grow back faster than if you were using creams or lotions? Shaving does, however, make your regrowth feel more prickly as the hair has been sliced off at an angle. Creams and lotions, on the other hand, dissolve the hair, making the regrowth softer. Normal Caucasian hair growth rate is 1–1.25cm every twenty-eight days.

Hop on the scales OR measure your waist?

If you're watching your weight and step on the scales in the morning, might you be better off reaching for the tape measure to work out if you're piling on the pounds? Scientists are studying this intensively because of international concerns over obesity and the results can be confusing.

One way to assess whether or not you're overweight is to calculate the Body Mass Index (BMI) — your weight in relation to your height. To work it out, divide your weight in kilos by your height in metres squared (or use imperial measures). Several websites do this for you — just Google 'BMI'. A BMI of between 18.5 and 25 indicates a healthy weight.

Some doctors argue that waist circumference is the more useful standard by which to judge excess weight: 'fat around the middle' is the real danger sign. A fat tummy is likely to have fatty organs underneath it, which, particularly for the liver, can be dangerous.

While a March 2011 study by British doctors, for example, disagreed with this, a more recent one in June 2011 in the US said that waist measurement is a more reliable indicator of obesity-related problems like heart disease and diabetes: anything above 80cm (31.5 inches) for women and 94cm (37 inches) for men increases the risk. Not sure where your waist is? Find the top of your hip bone and the bottom of your ribs and wrap the tape around the halfway mark, near your belly button.

Which method to choose? To calculate your BMI you have to be good at mental arithmetic or have access to an online calculator. Alternatively, just admit that your jeans really are getting tighter and reach for a tape measure. Both will help you work out if you need to lose weight, but I know which I find easier.

ANSWER: waist circumference

Mouthwash OR floss?

Mouthwashes taste refreshing and are easy to use, but there is little evidence that they improve dental health, although those containing chlorhexidine, an antiseptic, can alleviate some infections. They should be used only for short periods, however, as they may stain your teeth. There is some evidence that mouthwash may help improve bad breath temporarily, and the rinsing and spitting motions will clear out little bits of debris after brushing.

Flossing is universally recommended by dentists for removing plaque and bacteria, and mouthwash is no substitute. Use floss in a circular motion — don't saw up and down, which may damage your gums. Try the interdental brushes available from pharmacies if you find flossing tricky. It's good to floss at least once a day, preferably before going to bed, but morning will do if you forgot to floss the previous evening.

ANSWER: floss

Manual OR electric toothbrush?

There is nothing intrinsically bad about a manual toothbrush. According to the British

Dental Association, it's the way you brush your teeth that counts: use small circular motions. An electric toothbrush makes this much easier, and if you buy one with a timer you're more likely to keep going for the recommended two minutes' minimum brushing time. An overview of studies by the Cochrane Collaboration (a respected international body that systematically reviews health research), comparing electric toothbrushes, suggests that those using rotation oscillation (where the brush head rotates in one direction, then the other) reduce gum inflammation and help with plaque removal. Some dentists recommend that the under-tens stick to the manual type unless they are supervised: alone, they may just whiz the toothbrush around their mouths, defeating the object of cleaning each tooth slowly. That's the worst of both worlds.

ANSWER: electric

Regular OR whitening toothpaste?

Toothpaste manufacturers make all sorts of claims for their products but there isn't really a lot to choose between them. Whitening toothpastes are more abrasive than other kinds, and while they might cause a slight improvement in some people, they can damage the teeth. The essential ingredient in toothpaste is decay-preventing fluoride, especially if you live in an area where there are low levels in the water supply. In the UK, you can check this on DEFRA's website. Home whitening treatments are available, but they usually contain bleach and must be used with care. If you really want to whiten your teeth, it's best to see a dentist.

ANSWER: regular

Did you know?

. . . that fluoride is an extremely powerful chemical that can damage children's teeth before they emerge, causing dental fluorosis? The resulting stains disfigure the teeth and are not treatable except by cosmetic dentistry in adulthood. Manufacturers make fruit-flavoured toothpaste to encourage little ones to brush, but only a tiny amount of fluoride is needed to protect teeth from decay, so it is essential that small children spit it out rather than swallowing it: the damage is caused internally before the teeth emerge, not on their surface.

Spray, roll-on OR stick deodorants and anti-perspirants?

Anti-perspirants and deodorants come in many forms and do different jobs. Deodorant deals with the smell that skin bacteria create in our armpits; anti-perspirants do the same, in addition to preventing you from sweating. If you are not a very sweaty person, a deodorant should do the job. One Danish study suggested that the fragrance in deodorant is more likely to cause allergic reactions than those in other products, in which case it might be best to go for a brand that uses plant-based rather than chemical fragrances, or opt for a fragrance-free type.

Anti-perspirants are thought to work by blocking the skin's pores, mainly through the use of aluminium salts. Health scares about them also seem largely unfounded, although some of the aluminium products cause yellow stains on clothes. Look for brands with a small amount of aluminium or none. If the thought of chemicals on your skin bothers you, try a brand that uses natural ingredients, available from health-food or organic stores.

Spray deodorants and anti-perspirants used to have a bad name because the spray mechanism contained CFCs (chlorofluoro-carbons), which contribute to the depletion of the ozone layer, a protective barrier from the sun's harmful rays. But CFCs were banned in 1994 and are no longer a cause for concern. Alarm bells also rang when deodorants and anti-perspirants were linked to breast cancer, but that has been knocked on the head by several reliable overviews of the research.

The disadvantage of sprays, as anyone with a teenage son who has just started using them will attest, is that they are less accurate — hence the overpowering smell in the bathroom. They are also bulky and subject to airline baggage controls, which can be annoying when you go on holiday. Roll-ons, said by the NHS to be more effective than sprays, tend to be a little messy and may take longer to dry, so the risk of residual marks on your clothes is high.

Stick (or solid) varieties — which look a little like a giant lipstick and are now the most popular type in the US — avoid many of the drawbacks of sprays and roll-ons and, in my experience, have no drawbacks at all. They're widely available in supermarkets and pharmacies, and look out for brands containing natural ingredients in health-food stores.
ANSWER: stick

Moisturizer and foundation with OR without sun protection?

Cosmetics which contain sun protection may sound like a gimmick, especially if you live in a colder climate, but it's important to be aware of the strength of the sun's ultraviolet (UV) rays as these are the ones which cause us damage.

UVA rays are present all year round, even if you live a long way from the equator. They damage skin beneath the surface layer, which leads to ageing and can increase the risk of skin cancer. UVA protection is indicated with stars — look for four at least.

UVB rays peak during the summer months and can cause sunburn, ageing and skin cancer. So it's a good idea to use cosmetics that contain a sun protection factor of SPF 15 or more to protect against these harmful rays. This is no substitute for the stronger type of sun protection needed in the summer on holiday, for example, but every little helps.

(For more on sun protection see Lunch on page 88)

ANSWER: with sun protection

Moisturize morning OR night?

There's plenty of science to back the use of moisturizers, which help keep the surface layers of the skin hydrated with oil — and water-based emulsions. But is it best to use them by day or at night? Both types do the same job, and your age, skin type and the environment in which you spend most of your time will dictate which works best for you. Bear in mind that night creams tend to be heavier and may clog your pores — unhelpful if you're prone to spots, but if you like using them and feel they work, there's no reason not to. Beware the mantra: 'Your skin repairs itself at night.' Yes, our bodies need sleep, but there is nothing special about what your skin does at night. Its natural renewal process takes place around the clock. Some day creams offer sun protection and act as a good base for make-up, so if you're going to apply moisturizer just once a day, it's probably best to do it first thing in the morning.
ANSWER: morning

Getting Dressed

Oh, the pain and fury that can be unleashed by the simple question: 'What should I wear?' One tip everyone should know is: whatever you wear — decide the night before.

Tights OR stockings?

If you aren't prone to bouts of vaginal thrush (candidiasis), skip this entry and wear whatever you like. But if you do get thrush, a very common yeast infection that causes a creamy white discharge and intense itching, stockings may help. (They may also make you feel sexier.) Yeasts thrive in warmth and humidity — just the conditions created by tights, tight-fitting jeans or pants, especially if they contain nylon. Thrush can be treated with over-the-counter creams (it's important to continue using them for several days after the symptoms disappear), but if you have more than three or four bouts in a year, ask your GP to check what might be causing it. Some women find eating live natural yogurt helps, or inserting it on a tampon, but there is no substantial evidence to back this up.
ANSWER: stockings

Heels OR flats?

Flat shoes may seem more sensible than heels, but that isn't necessarily the case. Ballet-style pumps are fashionable but offer little support for the foot, and the lack of a strap can force the toes to 'claw' to stop the shoes slipping off. The UK Society of Chiropodists and Podiatrists recommends Mary-Jane style flats with a strap; or for heels try strappy Gladiator styles. Heels should be firm and thick for shock absorption, and shoes should have a supportive arch to keep the foot in place.

At the other extreme, very high heels shorten the calf muscles and women who wear them all the time can find switching to trainers or bare feet difficult and painful. The higher the heel, the greater the pressure on the ball of the foot, causing anything from blisters, corns and calluses to serious foot, knee and back pain. There's nothing like a pair of sexy high heels to help women feel more confident and glamorous, but the Society advocates changing shoe type and heel height from day to day. For everyday use, keep your heel height to about 3–5cm.

ANSWER: 3–5cm heels

Did you know?
. . . that in cultures where people don't wear shoes, deformities such as claw and hammer toes are non-existent?

EXPERT OPINION

Leading fashion writer Jess Cartner-Morley has an excellent tip for saving time while deciding what to wear in the morning: choose your outerwear first, even though it's the last thing you put on. If it's a wet, cold day when you will be out and about, opt for boots and a mac or coat, then choose what works with them to go underneath. A day of important meetings might mean a pair of smart heels and your best jacket. It's much easier to work out the details of which blouse, jumper or skirt completes the look than getting dressed and realizing you don't have shoes or a coat to go with what you've put on.

Something Extra

If you've been organized enough to get yourself and your family ready without any hiccups, what to do with any spare time you might have left?

Exercise in the morning OR evening?

Finding time to exercise often seems impossible when you lead a busy life, but if you want to get fitter or lose weight, you need to speed up your metabolic rate — the rate at which your body burns energy — and getting hot and sweaty is a good sign. When you exercise, your metabolic rate 'spikes', then gradually returns to its basal (resting) level quite slowly, burning calories for several hours. Leading fitness coach Matt Roberts suggests eating breakfast, then exercising an hour or so later for thirty minutes: then your body will have had time to digest the food. The free NHS podcast *Couch to 5k* is a gentle way to start running. See nhs.uk/livewell for details.

As an exercise early bird, you're less likely to be diverted by things during the day that scupper your plans to go to the gym, the pool or out for a run. Sleep experts also advocate exercise earlier rather than later, as physical activity stimulates your body and can make it harder to get off to sleep. But if you can't manage this, don't use it as an excuse to do nothing: your metabolic rate will slow down and burn calories less efficiently. Exercise at any time of the day is better than none.
ANSWER: in the morning

Should children watch TV in the morning OR later?

One study found that the children of working mothers spent more time watching TV than those of stay-at-home mothers. No surprise there, as anyone who struggles to juggle work and family commitments would probably agree. But ask any child-psychology expert or well-organized parent how they get themselves to work and the kids to school on time, and the 'one-eyed babysitter' will not be the answer. It's a team effort, and even small children can contribute by learning how to dress themselves, or older ones by making a packed lunch and finding their sports kit. Letting them watch TV may lead to squabbles over the choice of programme and tantrums when a parent switches off in the middle of what they're watching.

To save yourself a lot of hassle in the morning, organize the night before what you all need to get off to a flying start the next day.

ANSWER: later

Breakfast Time

It's sometimes said that breakfast is the most important meal of the day — but the manufacturers of breakfast cereals and other such products say it loudest: they're keen to fill us up with what are often sugary, starch-based products. Nevertheless, it is important to eat something soon after waking. Most nutritionists agree that eating nothing before lunch leaves blood-sugar levels low and reduces concentration.

Research also suggests that those who don't eat breakfast are more likely to gain weight. So, breakfast is a good idea — but what should you eat and drink? This chapter will help you cut through the myriad choices, at home and on the way to work. If you really can't face food first thing, try making yourself a peanut-butter or lean ham sandwich on wholegrain bread to take to work, or at least grab a banana. Another healthy — and cheap — option is to keep a packet of low-sugar, wholegrain cereal at work if possible, plus some milk and/or yogurt and juice in the fridge if you have access to one. This can help ward off the mid-morning temptation of fatty, sugary coffee-shop or vending-machine offerings.

What to Drink

Sometimes it's the first choice you make in the morning: tea or coffee? It's a personal decision, but here are a few facts to help.

Caffeinated OR decaffeinated drinks?

Too much caffeine can give you the jitters and stop you sleeping: it raises your heart rate and may even give you palpitations. But as anyone who can't get out of bed in the morning without a cuppa knows, it also stimulates the central nervous system: coffee or tea (black, green or white) will give you a little boost that can help you stay alert at the start of the day. A study published by Harvard scientists in September 2011 found that women who drink two to three cups of coffee per day are less likely to suffer from depression.

There are no official guidelines for caffeine consumption in the UK — except that pregnant women should stick to 200mg a day because a high caffeine intake has been associated with miscarriage. Those who suffer from high blood pressure or anxiety should also steer clear. How much is right for you is, of course, up to you, but diet experts suggest four or five caffeinated drinks per day, and that you should have the last one in the afternoon.

But do remember to bear in mind the different strengths of caffeinated drinks. An official UK survey of caffeine levels in drinks ranged from 1mg for the weakest tea to 254mg for the strongest cup of ground coffee. Don't forget drinks like cola and chocolate or guarana all contain caffeine.

ANSWER: caffeinated

Did you know?
. . . how much caffeine is in each of the following?

one mug of instant coffee	100mg
one mug of filter coffee	140mg
one mug of tea	75mg
one can of cola	40mg
one can of energy drink	80mg
one 50g bar of dark chocolate	around 50mg
one 50g bar of milk chocolate	around 25mg

(Source: bbc.co.uk)

Freshly squeezed OR juice from concentrate?

If you're confused by all the juice options available, here's the lowdown:

- Juice from concentrate is made by pasteurizing the squeezed juice (heat-treating to remove harmful bacteria), and evaporating most of the water content. The concentrate is then frozen and water is added later to make it up again into juice.

- Juice that's labelled 'not from concentrate' is not reduced but is pasteurized.

- Freshly squeezed juice is not pasteurized — or only slightly — which is why it has to live in the fridge as soon as you buy it, and has a shorter shelf life.

Health-food fanatics argue that any form of processing like concentrating or pasteurizing causes loss of nutrients from the juice, and that is true, up to a point. If you can afford to buy the freshly squeezed kind or have time to squeeze your own in the mornings, go ahead, but juices made from concentrate are a healthy, convenient and cheaper choice. Lots of health claims are made for different juices but the basic rule is: drink only one 150ml glass a day. In excess, because of its high sugar and acid content, it's fattening and bad for your teeth. Go for juices based on a single type of fruit: the blended varieties may be bulked up with the more sugary fruits, such as banana or apple. Only the varieties that say they are 100 per cent juice are free of additives — including sugar.

ANSWER: from concentrate

What to Eat

There are so many choices to make in the supermarket — usually when you're in a hurry and need a quick solution. But breakfast is one meal you can get right very easily.

Cereal OR eggs?

If you want an easy breakfast, cereal is probably the quickest option, but eggs, whether boiled, poached, scrambled or fried in a dash of oil, are also fast food. Which is best for your health? Eggs are low-calorie, protein-rich and a good source of vitamins

and nutrients. Although they contain cholesterol, it's not the potentially harmful kind,
and contrary to popular wisdom, there are no
guidelines on the number you can eat.
Cereal, on the other hand, may be full of
sugar — even so-called 'healthy' options such
as granola and raisin bran. If you choose it,
stick to the wholewheat varieties, with no
added sugar, and always check the box for
added ingredients. Or save yourself the
detective work: put your egg into a pan and
cover it with cold water, then bring it to the
boil while you pop a slice of wholegrain bread
into the toaster. Boil the egg for one or two
minutes — depending on how soft you like
them — and spread the toast with a little
olive or sunflower spread, cut up and use as
soldiers.
ANSWER: eggs

Multigrain OR wholegrain?

Bread, cereals, pasta and rice are often made
with grains whose outer layers have been
removed, leaving only the central starchy
part, known as refined carbohydrate. It is an
important source of energy, but health
professionals urge us to choose wholegrain
(or wholemeal) sources of carbohydrate

because they are more nutritious. Bran, the outer layer of the grain, is rich in fibre and stops the digestive system clogging up, while the inner layer — the germ — is rich in nutrients. The label 'multigrain' or 'seeded' may sound as if it is full of these goodies, but it means very little. A loaf of multigrain bread might be made from refined flour with some grains or seeds thrown in, whereas wholegrain bread or cereal should contain a majority of wholegrain products.

ANSWER: wholegrain

Did you know?

. . . that a pint of low-fat milk (which includes semi-skimmed, 1 per cent and skimmed) contains 100 per cent of our daily requirement for bone-promoting calcium? In fact, low-fat milk contains slightly more calcium than whole milk, and just as much protein to help you feel full for longer and build muscle. If you find skimmed milk too thin and watery, try the 1 per cent fat variety, which has less fat than semi-skimmed at 1.7 per cent.

Probiotic OR regular yogurt?

All types of yogurt contain 'live' bacteria, but not all types contain probiotics — 'friendly bacteria' that help keep our guts healthy, and a healthy gut is important to our overall well-being. Probiotics are mostly found in dairy products — look out for *Lactobacillus* or *Bifidobacterium* on the label. Probiotics seem to help sufferers with diarrhoea and irritable bowel syndrome; less convincing are claims that they may influence auto-immune conditions like asthma.

While there isn't yet any evidence to show whether probiotics are better taken as part of our daily diet or as supplements, it is clear they need to be taken very regularly — the odd tub of probiotic yogurt won't make much difference. However, as yogurt is also quite high in protein and calcium, it's a healthy choice, as long as the variety you select isn't too full of saturated fat or added sugar — so there's no problem in making it a regular part of your diet.

Probiotics are often talked about in conjunction with prebiotics, a form of carbohydrate found in some fruit and vegetables, which help promote the growth of probiotics in the gut. Again, there is some research to suggest they can help with digestive problems. Add some chopped banana to probiotic yogurt and you'll get some prebiotics into the bargain.

ANSWER: probiotic

Normal OR reduced-fat peanut butter?

Peanut butter is a good thing to put on your toast at breakfast, and because it is relatively high in protein, it will keep you going for longer than jam or honey. Although peanuts are not actually nuts but rather from the legume family, like chickpeas and lentils, they contain monounsaturated fats, a healthy kind of fat, and lots of nutrients. As a 20g serving of peanut butter is worth only about 50 calories, the brands with no added salt or sugar make a good breakfast spread, especially on a slice of wholegrain toast. Surely reduced fat must be healthier? Not necessarily. Food manufacturers who reduce fat in their products may make up for the loss of taste with cheap sweeteners, such as maltodextrin. Instead of reaping the benefits peanuts offer, you're consuming empty carbs and more sugar.

ANSWER: normal peanut butter

Spreads OR butter?

A 40g serving of butter — about a finger's width of a 250g block — contains the whole 20g daily allowance of potentially cholesterol-raising saturated fat for women, along with a rather substantial 300 calories. Ghee, used in cooking from the Indian subcontinent, is also high in saturated fat. While they are also high in calories, sunflower and olive oil contain healthier polyunsaturated and monounsaturated fats. If you can't resist butter, keep it at room temperature because it's easier to spread and you'll use less. Or else buy a spreadable version, which contains oil to make it softer.

ANSWER: spreads

Toast and Nutella OR pain au chocolat?

The chocolate-and-hazelnut spread Nutella sounds like a naughty treat, but a couple of slices of wholegrain toast with a heaped teaspoon contain about 280 calories — roughly the same as a Starbucks pain au chocolat, for example. These melt in the mouth so deliciously because they consist of fat, refined carbohydrate and sugar. Wholegrain toast with Nutella supplies more fibre, protein and nutrients so will keep you going for longer.

ANSWER: toast and Nutella

Muesli OR granola?

They both sound healthy — but beware: muesli and granola are pretty high in calories as they may contain a lot of added sugar, and nuts, which are high in fat. While both muesli and granola contain lots of healthy raw ingredients such as oats, seeds, nuts and dried fruit, granola packs in extra calories and fat because the ingredients are coated in a mixture of oil and sugar or syrup, and then baked — so it's better to stick to muesli.

If you are shop-buying, check the ingredients and go for brands where the amount of sugar and nuts is low. Sandwich chains sell granola with yogurt and fruit puree added. Again, these tempting little pots pack a big fatty calorific punch. At one UK chain, the Bircher muesli contains 304 calories and 9.7g of fat, and their granola with yogurt contains 579 calories and 20g of fat.

ANSWER: muesli

Health Supplements

Cranberry juice OR a supplement?

Cystitis is a painful urinary tract infection (UTI) that can, if left untreated, end in hospitalization. Cranberry juice and capsules are reputedly an effective cure. The theory is that a compound in the berries stops the offending bacteria clinging to the walls of the bladder. In October 2012 the Cochrane Collaboration suggested that while cranberry juice helps prevent UTIs in a few cases, it needs to be drunk in large quantities (150ml twice a day) to make a difference. Other cranberry products such as supplements were also found to be ineffective. However, drinking lots of fluids can help reduce the occurrence of UTIs, and a glass of cranberry juice counts as one of your five-a-day, so it's definitely worth a try if you suffer from cystitis. Frequently recurring cystitis may need treatment with antibiotics.
ANSWER: juice

Did you know?

. . . that green tea, orange juice and blueberries are high in antioxidants? These nutrients are thought by some people to 'mop up' harmful substances called free radicals: they occur naturally in the chemical processes in our bodies, but are associated with diseases like cancer and Alzheimer's, and also ageing. Antioxidants are in fact found in many different types of food such as shellfish, nuts, fruit, vegetables and tea — especially green tea (see more in Pick-Me-Ups, page 73) — and also in supplements, though there is no evidence to prove that the latter have the same effect as those in food. Nobody would argue that our health does not benefit from a diet rich in fruit and veg, but scientists are not sure of the role that antioxidants play: the evidence on their cancer-busting properties is conflicting. Some studies suggest that antioxidants might promote the growth of cancer cells as well as inhibit them.

Fish-oil supplement OR a multivitamin?

There is a lot of confusing information about vitamins and supplements, which is hardly surprising when they're such big business — worth £675 million in 2009 in the UK. If you are reasonably fit and healthy, and eat a well-balanced diet with plenty of fresh fruit, vegetables, wholegrains, some dairy products and lean protein, it's probably not worth spending money on multivitamins. You can get the recommended daily amount (RDA) of 80mg of vitamin C from a large orange, for example. The B and C vitamins are water-soluble anyway, so your pricey supplement will mostly end up flushed down the loo. Other vitamins are stored in the body for longer: vitamin A especially can be harmful in excess of the RDA. (How much of the RDA a supplement contains is shown on the bottle or packet — for more information on RDAs see The Lowdown on Nutritional Information, page 187.)

Fish oil contains omega-3 fatty acids, which are essential to our health and can help lower blood pressure and cholesterol. Because they act as anti-inflammatories, they may also help alleviate painful joints. It has been suggested that omega-3s may improve brain function but as yet there is no conclusive evidence of this. While there is no RDA for fish oil, the official advice in the UK, for example, is to eat a portion of oily fish, such as salmon, sardines and mackerel, each week to get the benefit of omega-3s. Not many of us do that, so a supplement may be worth considering. But the different brands vary in strength and a low dose won't make much difference, so look for doses at the higher end of the range. Also, they can cause indigestion; some brands are processed to avoid that so shop around.

ANSWER: fish oil

EXPERT OPINION

'I take fish-oil capsules. In my view the data are very convincing for fish oil to reduce cardiovascular risk and that's why I take it.' Professor Edzard Ernst, emeritus professor of complementary medicine at the University of Exeter, UK.

Zinc OR echinacea for colds?

While there is some evidence to support the claim that plant-derived echinacea purpurea may help shorten the duration of a cold, research is swinging behind zinc as both shortening and preventing one, according to the Cochrane Collaboration. Zinc is a mineral that occurs naturally in many different foods — oysters are particularly rich in the mineral, as are red meat and poultry. You can also take a zinc supplement, although you would have to take it daily for

five months to notice any difference. Echinacea tablets work out cheaper.

ANSWER: zinc

Did you know?

... that, according to a recent paper in the
Archives of Internal Medicine, about 13 per cent of
papers published during a year in the highly
respected New England Journal of Medicine
amounted to reversals of previously accepted thinking? It usually takes about ten years for such a
reversal to take place.

Your Working Day

If you hate your daily commute, your job gets you down and your colleagues wind you up, drastic solutions may seem to be the answer. But there is plenty that you can do to take the stresses and strains out of the daily grind. Using your journey as a way to clear your head or get some exercise, managing your time (and especially your email inbox) better, improving your relationships with co-workers and keeping your energy levels up can all help to make your job more fulfilling and less frustrating.

Getting There

You might have little or no choice about how you travel to work, the daily commute by bus or train being something that has to be endured. But for those who do have some flexibility here are a few tips . . .

Walk OR cycle?

Cycling is a great way to kill two birds with one stone: get to work without the hassle of public transport, and exercise at the same time. How many calories you burn depends on how vigorously you cycle and how many hills you climb, but cycling at 10mph/16kph for fifteen minutes on the flat would use about ninety calories. If you live close enough, walking briskly for thirty minutes would burn about 160. The joy of walking is that you don't need any kit, like helmets and lights. And you won't worry about where to park your bike and whether it will be stolen or vandalized. Walkers' minds can wander more freely: you don't have to concentrate on fending off aggressive drivers in the way that cyclists do, and you can listen to your favourite tracks on your iPod to help you keep your speed up on the way in or to relax on the way home. I've tried cycling and walking to work in central London: iPods and bikes are not a good combination — cyclists need all their wits about them, especially in urban areas, where around 75 per cent of fatal or serious cycling accidents occur. And they can't carry an umbrella.

ANSWER: walk

Did you know?
. . . that walking briskly for at least thirty minutes a day for a year could lead to an annual weight loss of around 5.5kg (12lbs)? The British Dietetic Association suggests that when you're trying to lose weight, you should aim to burn at least 1,000 calories a week in extra activity. This equates to thirty minutes of brisk walking daily. 'Brisk' means that you should feel slightly breathless and a bit sweaty.

Cycle helmet OR bare head?

There has been a lot of debate about whether cyclists should wear helmets or not. Those who object to the practice argue that helmet wearers feel safer so take more risks, or that helmets put people off cycling in the first place, reducing the environmental and health benefits. But when it comes to the risk of death and head injury, the evidence is pretty conclusive: a systematic overview of studies by the Cochrane Collaboration concluded that, overall, cycle helmets decrease the risk of head injury by around 69 per cent and death by around 42 per cent.

ANSWER: wear a helmet

At Work

Whatever you do and wherever you work, switching on your computer and finding an inbox stacked with emails may well be the first thing you do each morning. Dealing with emails is now key to working efficiently and avoiding the stress that comes with feeling snowed under. There are a few golden rules for emptying inboxes, suggested by psychologists such as David Allen and Emma Donaldson-Feilder:

- Delete — you wouldn't keep all the post you've ever received so why do it with email? It's amazing how many emails you can delete without reading them.

47

- Obey the two-minute rule: if that's all it will take, reply straight away.

- File it: make folders to store emails you want to retrieve with subject headings such as 'reply later', 'action' or 'waiting' (i.e. you have to wait for input from someone else to make your reply), 'CVs', 'invitations'. If this is not something you do already, think about how you handle your emails and create your own personal folder system. Don't forget to check the folders later — set aside time to do this regularly.

- Unsubscribe: if your inbox is clogged with feeds from newsletters or updates you've subscribed to but never read, why are you still subscribing to them? It takes seconds to unsubscribe (see the two-minute rule above).

  Or . . .

- . . . switch to Twitter. Links to newsletters and updates are often available there. They won't clog your computer and can be much faster to digest and forward to fellow tweeters.

Email OR a conversation?

What did people do before email was invented? They talked. In some offices colleagues now communicate entirely by email even if they sit next to each other. Presumably they're too busy checking their inboxes to speak. In my experience these are not happy working environments. One Scottish study found that some people check their email thirty or forty times an hour, and some companies ban email at certain times to force colleagues to talk to each other or enable them to work without being distracted by the dreaded inbox. Of course, no one wants to be interrupted every few minutes by colleagues asking questions. And if you need to have a record of what is being said, email is useful. But there are good reasons to avoid it. It's hard to detect tone of voice in an email: you may think yours sounds light-hearted, but that may not come across to the recipient. If you ask someone a question face to face or by phone, you are much more likely to be answered straight away: your request won't sit unacknowledged in their inbox. Talking also avoids long email conversation strings that leave others out at crucial stages, or which risk everyone using the 'reply all' button and adding to the inbox influx. Conference calls are more efficient for complex decisions in which several people are involved. And getting up from your desk and walking to a colleague's work station or office is a great way to take a little break, stretch your legs and get to know each other better.

ANSWER: conversation

Tricky email: respond now OR later?

There can be few people who haven't regretted writing a grumpy email in the heat of the moment. One way to control your email urge is to listen to the voice in your head that's saying, 'Should I be sending this?' The answer is probably 'No'. Try asking a trusted colleague to read the email first and tell you what they think. Or let technology come to the rescue by installing an application like Boomerang, which lets you build in a time delay to sending an email and can retrieve it after it's been sent. Otherwise, the cheapest and easiest option when you're feeling a little riled is to step away from the computer and reply when you've had a chance to cool off. Your response is guaranteed to be much more measured.

ANSWER: later

Did you know?

. . . that you are more likely to hear the truth from a colleague via email than via other means of communication? A US study of how often students lied in all types of communication during one week found they were less likely to do so in email than face to face, during phone calls or in texts. It's thought that, because emails are recorded, you fear you may be found out.

Managing Your Time

If you are overwhelmed by the amount of work you have to do, try breaking it into manageable chunks. The 1920s Russian psychologist Bluma Zeigarnik found that, once we start a task, our brains are more likely to recall it, so we have a better chance of completing it than if we never start it at all. This echoes the belief of leading work-life management guru David Allen: 'It's when you wind up not having done that which you've agreed with yourself should be done that the trouble begins.' Here are three ways in which psychologists recommend managing your workload:

- Make a list, either one big one or separate ones for different projects, or according to the urgent/important matrix format below.

- Prioritize: group tasks into four categories: urgent and important, not urgent but important, urgent but not important, and neither urgent nor important. This will point to what needs doing first. If everything seems urgent and important, try to take on less and delegate more.

- Ask yourself what is the worst that can happen if you don't complete the task on time, and how you will deal with your failure to do so. It will calm you down and help put things into perspective.

Perfectionism OR good enough?

Wanting to do the best you can is a laudable trait. But perfectionism, taken to extremes, isn't always the best recipe for success. According to Professor Randy Frost, a US psychologist who has studied the subject, perfectionists can be overly self-critical, and racked with self-doubt. They are often the children of parents who set very high standards and are highly critical of mistakes. It's great to have colleagues who set the pace for others and

pay immense attention to detail, but perfectionists can slow things down, miss deadlines, be
blind to the bigger picture and indecisive,
driving their co-workers (and bosses) nuts. A
former boss, a very high achiever, once told me,
when I was fretting over a detail, 'Don't let the
best be the enemy of the good.' It's sound advice.
ANSWER: good enough

Make one list OR several?

This is a hot topic among life coaches and
psychologists. Lists certainly help busy (and
scatty or forgetful) people to plan and prioritize. But should you make one long list or
several for different tasks? And how often
should you make them? And where? On paper,
on your PC or your mobile? Time-management
expert David Allen suggests that you keep a
master list with things on it like 'book holiday', 'hire new staff member', 'take car for
service', and that under those headings you
list the steps needed to finish each task. He
also likes easily updated digital calendars for
keeping track of when the steps have to be
taken. The advantage of making lists on an
electronic device is that you can update them
more easily on the move than with pen and
paper (standing on a railway platform or sitting

on the bus, say), and if you are a multi-list-maker, you are less likely to lose them than if they are on lots of different bits of paper. The trouble with several lists, however, is that they are harder to keep track of.

If you find making lists useful, then do it in the way that works best for you — i.e. as a genuine aid to getting things done on time. As a compulsive list-maker, I'd suggest a compromise at work: start a new to-do list every week, and highlight what's top priority (see Managing Your Time, page 51), or make a note of which day it must be done by. You can carry over any unfinished jobs to the next week's fresh list.

ANSWER: make one list

Keep focused OR daydream?

If you've ever said 'My brain hurts' when you've been concentrating on the same challenging task for a long time, it's not far from the truth. Neuroscientists like Jonah Lehrer think the rational decision-making part of the brain becomes depleted if it's overused; 'switching off' and daydreaming help to mingle thoughts and ideas from different parts of the brain so that we think more creatively. It's why we

often have a 'Eureka!' moment while staring mindlessly out of the window or doing the dishes. Just don't do it all day.
ANSWER: daydream

Delegate OR do it yourself?

Do you often feel resentful because you seem to be doing much more than everyone else? If your role at work involves managing other people, maybe you could learn to delegate more effectively. Tasks that you can't accomplish in two minutes (following management expert David Allen's rule) can either be handed on to someone else or deferred until you have time to tackle them. If you're delegating, make sure that colleagues understand clearly what's expected of them, and perhaps agree, or make a note to yourself, to follow up later with them. In bigger organizations it may be helpful for each department to set up an online document that lists who is expected to do what; at the end of the week everyone enters what they have actually done. You don't need a management expert to tell you that showing your appreciation of a task well done, or offering constructive feedback when it isn't, will sharpen your ability to delegate.

ANSWER: delegate

Did you know?

. . . about the praise sandwich? This tip was given to me by a highly respected publishing executive when she was explaining how to get someone to rewrite an article. It applies to many situations in which you have to reject an idea, or persuade someone to have another go. Start by saying something positive, then deliver the bad news, and finish with a second positive comment — the bad news is sandwiched between positive feedback. For example: 'Thanks, I really like your article. You've clearly done a lot of research and the bit about X is really interesting. But the style isn't quite right for us and it's a bit longer than I expected. It's a little too academic-sounding. I wonder if you could cut it down a bit and make it slightly lighter? We'd really like to run it and I don't think it'll take you too long.'

Meet with colleagues OR work independently?

If there's one aspect of office life that's more time-consuming than dealing with emails, it's meetings. Some days are entirely taken up with them, leaving little time to get on with your work, which creates anxiety and frustration. But are two heads always better than one? Some interesting research has been done into brainstorming, suggesting the opposite: experiments showed that individuals working on their own produce more high-quality ideas than those working in groups. 'People who like meetings are those who don't enjoy getting things done,' says psychology writer Oliver Burkeman, in *Help! How to Become Slightly Happier and Get a Bit More Done*. It's thought that this happens because of the 'bystander effect': people in groups care less about outcomes than those working alone, who know that they are entirely responsible for their results.

If a meeting is being held to update the participants on progress, could this be achieved more effectively by email or on the phone? But of course, a well-run meeting can be very productive, and when so many of us communicate via the Internet or the phone, it's also important to meet colleagues face to face: it reminds us that we're part of a team.

ANSWER: work independently

Did you know?

. . . if you have to attend meetings and want to boost your chances of gaining influence, one study suggests employing the 'centre-stage effect' and sitting in the middle? That's where the important people in a group are usually found (think of wedding photos). The ones at the sides are more likely, literally, to be bystanders.

Say yes OR no?

If you feel so overloaded that it's making you anxious and irritable, or disrupting your sleep, perhaps you're trying to please too many people too much of the time. Psychologists believe that such behaviour is rooted in childhood. If parents control children too tightly and only make them feel loved if they do as they're told, the children grow up with an undeveloped sense of what they want for themselves and look to other people for approval. Self-help writer Elizabeth Hilts even identifies a (mostly female) trait called 'toxic niceness', resulting from the fear of confrontation. At work these people say yes to everything to please colleagues — and often fail to deliver because they have taken on too much.

At worst, people-pleasers go along with the

wishes and demands of others, then explode when it all gets too much. Of course it's important to be sensitive to people's needs but not at the expense of your own. Hilts even recommends getting in touch with your 'inner bitch'. Nina Grunfeld, founder of the self-development organization Life Clubs, recommends making a list with two columns, the one on the left headed 'I'm saying No to . . . ', and the one on the right headed, 'Which means I'm saying Yes to . . . ' It's a helpful technique for working out your priorities and not coming across to your boss as unwilling: 'Sorry, I won't be able to come to the meeting but I will be able to finish the report you wanted by this evening.'

ANSWER: say no (nicely)

EXPERT OPINION

'The degree to which you feel good about what you're doing is equal to the degree that you know what you're not doing, and have made that OK.' David Allen, *Getting Things Done*.

Getting Along with your Colleagues

Let's face it, we all have workmates with whom we don't exactly 'hit it off' at all times. But it doesn't have to be confrontational.

Blame others OR move on?

When something goes wrong at work it's natural to get annoyed with colleagues if you feel they've messed up. But should you point the finger or keep quiet? When you blame others you're making yourself the injured party and setting yourself up as their victim. If a shared desk, for example, is untidy, and you blame the colleague you share it with, you're putting them in a position to upset you and giving them power in the relationship. Then you might blame yourself for 'letting' them do this to you. But blaming yourself is also a total waste of time. Nina Grunfeld suggests that if you feel bad about something, forgive yourself and get on with your life. Ask yourself what you can learn from having done it 'wrong'. Perhaps to feel more in control of a situation such as the untidy desk, you could suggest a weekly tidy-up session when you sort out the mess together.

ANSWER: move on

Apologize OR say nothing?

We all make mistakes, and there's not much point in drawing attention to the ones no one else will notice. But if it's a serious mistake, saying nothing comes across as arrogant and immature, like a child who can't face up to what they've done. A perfunctory 'sorry' might make things worse if it sounds insincere. A study by US psychologists at the University of Maryland suggested there were three types of apology: compensation ('I'm sorry I forgot to do those figures. I'll stay late and get them done'); empathy ('I'm sorry I didn't ask you to the meeting. You must feel as if I don't value your opinion when I do'); and acknowledgement of violated rules/ norms ('I'm sorry I told X about the proposed merger. It was a breach of confidentiality').

The trick is to match the type of apology to the wronged party. Someone who values relationships, for example, will probably respond best to an empathetic apology. A mixture of all three types is probably the most effective way to sound as if you really mean it. Studies suggest it's a good idea to get it over

with: people who 'fess up sooner rather than later come across as more likeable.
ANSWER: apologize

Accept OR try to change decisions?

When a painful decision comes down from on high that you don't agree with, is it best to keep your head down or to try to voice your objections? It's probably worth asking yourself how much, realistically, you can influence the situation. Getting upset about things you can't control, like a new boss, restructuring or a round of redundancies, can be distracting and pointless. If that's how you always react to decisions you don't like, you'll soon make yourself unpopular with managers who may be implementing decisions they don't like either. What you can influence is the way you react to the situation: maybe the changes could work out better for you in the long run. There's plenty of research to back up the view that optimists are better at dealing with setbacks, and are possibly healthier because their upbeat outlook may influence their immune system. People who resist change are often anxious types. Ask yourself what you're afraid of and what steps you can take to get back in control, such as looking for a new job,

updating your CV, or starting a professional profile on a networking site like LinkedIn.
ANSWER: accept

Pass on gossip OR keep quiet?

The latest tittle-tattle about goings-on in the workplace can certainly perk up a dull day, but beware of being its source. If you've ever felt suspicious of a gossip and wondered if they talk about you like that behind your back, it's down to a process psychologists call 'spontaneous trait transference'. Experiments show that the listener unconsciously associates some of the negative things they are hearing about someone else with the person who's telling them. So, as my mother used to say, 'If you can't say anything nice, don't say anything at all.'
ANSWER: keep quiet

Make tea and coffee for yourself OR for everyone?

If you're the sort of jolly person who always offers to make or fetch tea or coffee for colleagues as well as for yourself, don't expect undying gratitude. Psychological experiments have found that little favours or kind gestures are most appreciated by strangers, who will often give more in return. Favours don't go down well if an ulterior motive is suspected. While it's of course nice to make the occasional cup of tea or coffee for your colleagues, if you do it a lot, and have ever felt resentful of those who don't make one for you in return, could it be that your real motive for making tea and coffee for others is to feel appreciated?

ANSWER: for yourself

Pick-Me-Ups

If you feel your energy dipping during the day, it's tempting to boost it with a trip to the coffee-vending machine or by munching a chocolate bar or packet of crisps. While there's nothing wrong with a little caffeine boost or treat during the day, relying on caffeine and sugar to get you through is a sign of an unhealthy diet and bad eating habits. Perhaps you skip breakfast or lunch (see suggestions for fast, healthy options on page 30 and page 78), consume lots of calorie- and caffeine-packed coffee-shop drinks, or don't take enough breaks to move around, clear your head and get your blood flowing.

What to Eat and Drink

Here's the lowdown on how to keep going without piling on the pounds or spending a fortune in a coffee shop.

Latte OR cappuccino?

Want to know how to save 600 calories and almost your total daily saturated fat allowance (20g) in your coffee break? Swap a Starbucks venti whole milk white chocolate mocha with whipped cream (620 calories) for a venti Americano with some hot skinny milk (about 50 calories). That's an extreme example, but the amount that coffee-shop drinks have contributed to our weight gain in the last decade or so is not to be underestimated. A less exaggerated comparison would be to cut calorie intake in half by swapping a grande latte with semi-skimmed milk (150 calories) for a tall cappuccino with semi-skimmed milk (90 calories). The difference is explained by the amount of milk contained in proportion to water: a latte (which is Italian for 'milk') contains much more milk than a cappuccino (and an Americano or macchiato with a dash of milk contain even less). Of course milk is a nutritious drink but large, sweetened milky coffees arguably are not. Some coffee shops now show nutritional information on their websites, so do check them out if you want to compare one of your favourites and make a simple swap and cut down on calories.

(For caffeine intake, see Caffeinated or decaffeinated drinks?, page 27)
ANSWER: cappuccino

Did you know?

. . . that it's important to drink about 1.2 litres (six to eight glasses) of fluid per day? Whether this should include just water or other soft drinks has been the subject of endless debate, but most dieticians agree that it can include soft drinks and moderate amounts of tea or coffee. But just a large latte (223 calories), a can of soft drink (139 calories) and an afternoon cup of tea with a spoonful of sugar (34 calories) add up to almost 400 calories. Swapping the latte for a filter coffee or Americano, choosing a diet drink or sparkling water and cutting out the sugar would save about 300. If you want to save money, too, invest in a large, attractive bottle or carafe, fill it with tap water every day and make a rule to drink the lot by the time you go home.

Scone OR muffin?

If you skipped breakfast and are looking longingly at the delicious array of baked goods while your coffee's being made, what's the best choice? Even a healthy-sounding skinny blueberry muffin at Starbucks packs in 372 calories — more than a 58g Mars bar (260 calories), while their classic blueberry muffin has a whopping 481. Scones are generally among the least-worst offenders in the cake stakes because they contain relatively low amounts of fat and sugar, so at 252 calories the Starbucks plain scone with a scraping of jam or butter is a better choice. Add a piece of fruit and that's not a bad breakfast substitute.
ANSWER: scone

Fruit juice OR smoothie?

If the smoothie contains just fruit and no dairy produce, like milk or yogurt, there's not much to choose between it and plain juice, calorie-wise. A 250ml bottle of orange juice from one sandwich chain contains 114 calories and 28.6g of sugar, while a strawberry smoothie has 128 calories and 28g of sugar. While smoothies use crushed fruit rather than just juice, and contain a little more fibre, look out for the inclusion of bananas, which add bulk to more expensive fruit, like strawberries, and make the drink taste sweeter. The addition of milk or yogurt, as long as it's a plain, low-fat variety, can keep you going for longer without adding too many calories, because they contain fats and proteins. Bear in mind that smoothies count as one, or at a pinch two, of the recommended five-a-day fruit and veg.

ANSWER: smoothie

Smoothie OR fruit?

There's no contest here: a small 227g pack of strawberries plus a banana has about the same calories as a 250ml bottle of strawberry and banana smoothie from a well-known brand. Smoothies can lose some nutritional value in their manufacture, and only count as (at most) two of the recommended five daily portions of fruit and vegetables. So, for the same calorific content of a smoothie, you could get two healthier snacks by eating half

of the strawberries and banana, and saving the rest for later.
ANSWER: fruit

Orange OR kiwi?

If you like to snack on fruit, kiwis are one of the healthiest, containing about the same amount of vitamin C as an orange of the same size and more fibre than an apple. Peel and eat, or just slice off the top and scoop out the flesh with a spoon. (Children love eating them served like this in an egg cup — 'kiwi like a boiled egg', as it's known in our house.)
ANSWER: kiwi

Peanuts OR nuts and raisins?

Swap a 50g pack of roasted peanuts for a 45g bag of nuts and raisins and you'll save yourself at least 100 calories, 30g of fat, and a lot of salt. Another example of how little swaps can boost your nutritional intake during the day and lower the calorie count.
ANSWER: nuts and raisins

Did you know?

. . . that sitting in front of a computer screen can cause all sorts of aches and pains? To make sure you're sitting comfortably, ask yourself the following questions

- Are you taking a five-to-ten-minute break after fifty to sixty minutes' continuous screen and/or keyboard work?

- Are your eyes level with the top of the screen?

- Do you look up from your screen into the distance occasionally to avoid eye strain?

- Is your lower back straight and supported?

- Are your arms level with the surface of your keyboard — i.e. not at an angle?

- Are your upper legs at right angles to your upper body and lower legs?

- Are your feet flat on the floor or, if not, on a footrest?

- Can you operate the mouse with your wrist straight and your forearm supported?

The answer to all these questions should be yes.

Did you know?

. . . that despite all the claims for the disease-busting properties of green tea, the jury's still out? It is thought to fight cancer, thanks to substances it contains called catechins, which are supposed to inhibit the growth of cancer cells. But an overview of fifty-one studies by the Cochrane Collaboration found that the evidence was conflicting: there was some support for the theory with certain cancers, but not others. A less comprehensive review came to a similarly 'maybe' conclusion about green tea's possible role in preventing heart attacks. Beyond doubt, however, is that green tea has much less caffeine than black tea and coffee beans. The general message seems to be that drinking three to five cups a day (up to 1,200ml) is safe and might have possible benefits. But don't count on green tea alone as a life-saver.

Can of diet drink OR bar of chocolate?

If it's a caffeine kick you're looking for, there's about the same amount in a can of diet cola as there is in a small bar of dark chocolate (with at least 70 per cent cocoa solids). The diet cola is nutritionally worthless, so it hardly has any calories, while the chocolate (of course) contains sugar and saturated fat — a 35g bar is worth about 190 calories — so this is not a tip for weight watchers. The fat will keep you going for longer, however, and nutrients called flavonols, which are found in chocolate with a high cocoa content, might benefit heart health. But scientists don't really understand how this works and, of course, its fat and sugar content could cancel out them out. Sigh.

ANSWER: chocolate

Lunch

Millions of us eat our lunch sitting at our desks, working straight through the day without a proper break, or skip it altogether. In tough economic times, job insecurity is fuelling our need to be seen to get things done and, of course, sometimes the pressure of work makes it impossible to stop. But if this becomes a habit, it is damaging both physically and mentally.

What to Eat

What are the best ways to make light work of a quick, healthy lunch break?

Big lunch OR big supper?

When we eat, some of the digested food is converted into blood sugar (or glucose), which is a process regulated by the hormone insulin. Eating a lot makes us feel sleepy, scientists think, because brain cells that keep us alert are damped down by raised blood sugar after a meal. It could be an evolutionary response: once our ancestors had found their food and eaten it, it was time to sleep and conserve energy. Some foods, like pasta, which our bodies convert into blood sugar, make us sleepier than others. So, unless you're on holiday or it's the weekend, avoid a long, leisurely meal at lunchtime if you want to stay awake at work in the afternoon. Save the pasta for an evening when you really need a good night's rest.

ANSWER: big supper

Wrap OR baguette?

You've nipped out to grab something to eat but you're really peckish and need something a little more satisfying than a regular sandwich. A freshly baked baguette with your favourite filling is tempting. The wraps look good too, but as they've got more filling they must be more fattening, right?

In fact, wraps are an excellent choice for a sandwich-type meal because the proportion of filling to bread is high, and it's the filling that keeps you going, especially if you choose some lean protein like chicken with lots of crunchy salad and raw veg. Flatbreads have a lower GI (glycaemic index) value than baguettes, which means your body will burn the energy they give more slowly and you won't feel hungry again so soon. Unless the flatbreads are spread with butter, you're spared a lot of calories and saturated fat. At the time of writing, a chilli prawn salad crayfish wrap from one well-known sandwich chain, for example, is 298 calories, with 10g of fat, while their tuna mayo baguette has 484 calories and 22.9g of fat — almost a third of your daily allowance. Watch out for fatty dressings in wraps, though, like loads of creamy mayo.

ANSWER: wrap

Did you know?

. . . that a sandwich can provide a really healthy and light meal? Made with wholegrain bread and a scraping of butter, or sunflower or olive spread, lean protein such as ham or tuna, and packed with as much raw veg (like salad leaves, tomato and cucumber) as possible, sandwiches can contain all the food groups needed in a balanced diet: unrefined carbs, fruit and veg, protein and dairy fats.

Mayonnaise OR butter?

A thinly spread 7g serving of light mayo has about 23 calories and 2.3g of fat made from vegetable oils, while the same amount of butter has about 50 calories and 5g of saturated fat. Even regular mayo contains fewer calories. Butter is made from milk, and therefore contains a high amount of animal fat, which is high in saturated fat — the type that can raise cholesterol, which can be bad for your heart and cardiovascular system. Ask for your lunchtime sandwich to be spread with light mayo instead of butter, or try this at home if you make a packed lunch.
ANSWER: mayonnaise

Soup OR salad?

They both sound healthy — and if they're packed with veg, fruit and lean meat or fish, they can be. But watch out for salads with fatty dressings or lots of cheese, and soup loaded with cream, salt or fatty meat, like chorizo, to make it tasty, or bulked out with carbs like potatoes, pasta or rice. Of course you wouldn't want a steaming bowl of soup on a hot summer's day, but in winter soup is warming and comforting. And it can be more filling too — recent television research showed, with ultrasound scanners, how soldiers who ate a blended soup of rice, chicken, vegetables and water felt full for longer than those who had eaten the same ingredients as solid food, with a glass of water. Why? The blended food was bulkier so it couldn't pass through the stomach as quickly.

ANSWER: soup

Did you know?

. . . that many international food chains such as Subway and Burger King display the nutritional content of their products on their websites? Just Google the name of the chain and find the part of the site about their products and nutrition. You can bookmark the links for easy reference. McDonald's even include nutritional information on their food packaging. But it's too late once it's sitting in front of you to discover that your quarter-pounder with cheese, medium fries and a medium coke has 900 calories and about 40g of fat.

Sushi OR sashimi?

There are definite health benefits in eating these Japanese staples, which are now available in many fast-food outlets and supermarkets. They include omega-3 fatty acids, important for heart health and found in oily fish, like salmon and tuna, plus vitamins A, B, C and E and the trace element iodine in seaweed, essential for keeping our cells and metabolic rate healthy. Plain rice is also a good source of carbohydrate, and the small amount found in sushi won't leave you feeling over-full. Pregnant women should be wary of the mercury levels in deep-sea fish, such as tuna, limiting the amount of oily fish they eat; they should not eat raw shellfish at all. Official advice in the UK is that fish should be frozen before eating raw. Restaurants and shops that sell sushi have to do this by law to kill off any possibly harmful bacteria. So a good, light choice overall — but take care in restaurants with conveyor belts: it's easy to over-order.

There's not much to choose between sushi and sashimi, but the high proportion of rice to protein and veg in the sushi tips the balance for slimmers towards sashimi, which are pieces of raw or cured fish; perhaps order one or two sushi or a little rice and some vegetables, like raw edamame beans, on the side.

ANSWER: sashimi

Did you know?
. . . that it can take fifteen to twenty minutes after food is first eaten for the satiety signals to reach the brain? If you usually munch your lunch with your eyes on your email, try moving away from your work station and savouring what you're eating. It will help you slow down and consume less.

What to Drink

A big drink of water at lunchtime is a good idea: two-thirds of our body is made up of the stuff, and the suggested daily intake of fluid is about 1–1.5 litres a day. Although this can be made up of other drinks, they may not be as healthy as water — a fluid intake consisting only of coffee and fizzy drinks, for example, is probably not a good idea. And tap water is free.

Fizzy water OR still?

If you've been sitting in a stuffy office all day or running around doing chores, you may be dehydrated. This can make you feel sleepy and grumpy: our brains really need water to keep alert. But if you're buying a bottle to go with lunch or ordering in a restaurant, and have heard stories that fizzy drinks are bad for your health, what to do?

The bubbles in a bottle of fizzy water are created by the addition of carbon dioxide. Isn't that a nasty greenhouse gas that's contributing to our fears about global warming? And aren't fizzy drinks full of acid that destroys tooth enamel and rots bones? The amount of carbon dioxide in fizzy water is negligible and therefore unlikely to do you any harm. Tooth damage is associated with the sugar and acid in sweetened soft drinks or in fruit juice, not with the bubbles. So there's little to worry about — except one thing. The gas has to go somewhere — your digestive system — and the way it gets out can cause embarrassing social problems later in the day,

especially if you're prone to bloating.
ANSWER: still

Getting Out of the Office

There are several good reasons to get out of the office for a while in the middle of the day — one of which is simply to clear your head.

Exercise indoors OR go out?

Government guidelines exhort us to get active for at least 150 minutes a week. If your busy schedule makes this seem impossible, then even three ten-minute chunks each day will get your blood flowing and your muscles moving. A report in the medical journal *The Lancet* in July 2012 warned that approximately one third of adults worldwide are not physically active enough and that this is as risky as heart disease, diabetes, and breast and colon cancer. Try joining up with a colleague to help you stay motivated, or get a group together for a game of football or Frisbee in the park once a week. Plenty of studies support the idea that contact with nature is beneficial, from improving hospital

recovery rates to reducing antisocial behaviour and boosting creativity. If you can't get near a green space in your lunch break, buy yourself a pot plant or, if you're home-based, paint the walls a restful shade of green.
ANSWER: go out

Meet a friend OR eat alone?

If work is hectic and you have family and social commitments in the evening, a quiet lunch break may be the only time in the day you have to yourself. But it's easy to fall into a routine of doing the same thing at lunchtime — dashing to the shops, going to the same sandwich bar or the staff cafeteria.

Meeting friends or colleagues you don't often see is an important way of staying in touch with a wider social and professional network. Also, if things are getting you down in the office, sharing the problem can help. And if things go really pear-shaped, your professional network can be vitally important in helping you find a new job. If you work from home, 'doing lunch' can stop you getting 'cabin fever' and feeling out of touch.

A fascinating study of the most creative executives, published in the *Harvard Business*

Review in 2009, revealed that they were distinguished by excellent 'discovery skills': they were always seeking out new connections, ideas and experiences. They found networking with people from different backgrounds crucial in gaining new perspectives. So if Bill Gates can do it . . .
ANSWER: meet a friend

Swim OR run?

If you like to get out at lunchtime and are pretty fit, what's the best way to spend half an hour? Considerations such as how much kit you need, showers, cost and accessibility can potentially undo good intentions. If you want to keep it simple, very brisk walking (5mph) uses up to 250 calories in thirty minutes, the same as a game of singles tennis. Swimming vigorously burns up about 300 calories and is a great way to exercise your whole body, but it costs money and you have to build in time to get to the pool and to dry your hair afterwards. If you really want an efficient way to burn up calories, and you're lucky enough not to be concerned about your joints, running is hard to beat: at 8mph, it will use around 400 calories in thirty minutes — about the

amount you'd find in a hearty sandwich. So that's burning off lunch sorted.
ANSWER: run

Did you know?
... that your smartphone or computer can help you keep health goals on track with apps, tweets and websites? Many are free or cost only a few pence, and they're great if you're on the move. One of my favourite apps, Sleep Pillow, has lots of different soundtracks to help you get off to sleep, such as whale noises or gentle rainfall. Then there's the drinks tracker at nhs.uk, which helps you calculate how many units of alcohol you're drinking via a smartphone or your desktop. Plenty of websites, such as weightlossresources.co.uk, are full of information on the nutritional content of food and healthy eating; they also offer exercise tips. Look out for sites run by doctors, qualified health professionals or major health charities to avoid charlatans. Many have forums that you can join for moral support. Lots of health charities have Twitter feeds so that you can keep up with the latest tips and trends.

Did you know?
... that even five minutes' exercise every day can help you stay trim? It's best to target the areas

you're most concerned about: if it's your middle, try sit-ups; if you can stretch to ten minutes, do some lunges and squats to tone your lower body, too.

Sunscreen OR unprotected skin?

If you use your lunch break to get some exercise out of doors, good for you. However, the sun is at its strongest in the middle of the day, especially in summer, so think about applying some sunscreen. Recent research has established that we might be slapping on too much, though: some of us lack vitamin D, which our bodies make through direct exposure to sunlight and which is essential for all-round good health and growth, especially strong bones. So is it best to go without?

Doctors recommend two or three twenty-to-thirty-minute exposures to direct sunlight on bare arms and face each week in the summer months (April to September). Twenty to thirty minutes isn't very long, so unless you cover up routinely and stick to the doctors' advice, it's a good idea to apply sunscreen. Make sure you check the UVA protection factor (UVA is a type of ultraviolet sun ray), often displayed on the back of the bottle with star symbols. It's very important:

that's what protects you against possible skin cancer — a disease that's on the rise. Go for the highest possible number of stars.

Most products display the sun protection factor (SPF) on the front of the container: this shows how much protection it gives against burning, and which one you choose will depend on how fair your skin is and how much of a sun-kissed glow you're after. There are no official recommendations about how much to use or what type, but an SPF of fifteen is thought to be adequate. If in doubt, go for the highest.

ANSWER: sunscreen

Evenings Out

An evening out in good company, a meal at a lovely restaurant, a visit to the cinema or a great show are some of life's pleasures, especially after a stressful day at work, ploughing through chores at home or dealing with fractious children. You don't need a psychologist to tell you that having treats to look forward to gives you a valuable boost, or that good social networks help fight the blues, and that new experiences and situations are important for keeping your brain active. But evenings out can also become routine, and if that involves drinking like a fish after work, too many junk-food takeaways or boredom with the same old faces and places, your physical and mental health will suffer. Follow a few basic rules about food, drink and your social life, though, and you'll make the most of the precious hours of freedom after the daily grind.

What to Do

As many of us have to spend our working day sitting in front of a computer screen it's vital we make the most of any free time we get in the evenings. Whether it be meeting up with friends or trying something completely new, the possibilities are endless.

Do the same thing OR something new?

'Hedonistic habituation' is a delightful psychobabble phrase coined by US happiness researchers Ken Sheldon and Sonja Lyubomirsky, meaning that even if you really enjoy something you'll get bored with it after a while. They claim that people who initiate positive changes, like starting a new hobby or joining a club, remain happier for longer than those who have a significant change in circumstances, like getting a pay rise or a new car. Eventually the thrill of the latter wears off, but constant exposure to new experiences, people and ideas stimulates our minds and gives us new sources of pleasure. So, if you like going to the theatre and see mostly straight plays, why not try a musical or the opera — or even join a drama group? Just think — joining a book group is a great way of discovering not only a genre or author you've not previously encountered but also making new friends in the process. Alternatively, training for a triathlon can encourage you to get fit, to take up a new sport and to set yourself goals.

ANSWER: do something different

Old friends OR new?

If you're fond of your old mates but want to meet new people, or even a new partner, Andrew G. Marshall, psychologist and author of *The Single Trap*, has an interesting take on different types of friendship group. 'Bonding' groups are close-knit circles of old friends containing 'people like us' to whom we turn for ongoing support, reassurance and affection — like the women in *Sex and the City*. But such groups can, by their nature, be quite closed and they're unlikely to introduce you to anyone new. 'Bridging' groups are different: you'll find them at, for example, an evening class, sports club, or through your children's school. They bridge existing groups

of people, and are a great way to tap into new ones if you want to expand your social circle.
ANSWER: new ones

What to Eat and Drink

If you're off out for drinks, or to the cinema, and you fancy a little snack, the options are not always that healthy. Fear not, there's plenty you can eat and drink without compromising on taste and health benefits.

A sandwich OR yogurt to line your stomach?

If you've ever joined colleagues for a quick drink after work and found yourself still there hours later, much the worse for wear after drinking on an empty stomach, you'll know how that feels the morning after. Health professionals recommend that you grab something to eat to line your stomach before you drink alcohol, so a sandwich is fine (although make sure you go for something simple and nutritious like ham and tomato on wholegrain bread).

It's a good idea to keep something to hand at work for such occasions, such as a few crackers or unsalted nuts. If you have access to a fridge, then a glass of milk or some yogurt will line your stomach cheaply with relatively few calories; as the fats in dairy produce are digested quite slowly it will line your stomach for longer than a sandwich. Yogurt with probiotic live bacteria may even help your digestion.

ANSWER: milk or yogurt

Did you know?

. . . that juice-based soft drinks may sound healthy but often contain a fair amount of sugar? A 275ml bottle of J20 orange contains 132 calories, and colas typically provide about 140 in a regular 330ml bottle — plus the same amount of caffeine as half a cup of instant coffee. If you're happy that you have your drinking under control, you might be better off with a large measure of gin and slim-line tonic at about 120 calories. Skip the gin and you probably have the best soft-drink option, apart from water.

Sweet OR salted popcorn?

The food on offer at some cinema chains is a dietician's nightmare: ice cream, sweets, fizzy drinks, popcorn laden with fat and sugar, nachos and cheesy dips, all in monster portions. Popcorn is made from a type of maize that expands when it's heated. It's full of fibre, reasonably low in calories and pretty filling. But covered with butter, oil, salt or sugar it turns into a nutritional car crash. If you do indulge, brace yourself for the following information. According to one cinema's website, a large carton of sweet popcorn contains 869 calories, 29g of fat and 0.1g of salt. The salted kind has only slightly fewer calories at 812, about the same amount of fat and 4g of salt — almost the total recommended daily salt allowance. The least-bad option is a small portion of salted popcorn, which has about 360 calories and 13g of fat.

So, if you like to munch on a snack while you watch a film, why not avoid temptation and save a lot of money by taking your own treats, such as a small bar of chocolate (preferably 70 per cent cocoa solids or above) or a small packet of sweets or raisins, a bottle of fizzy water or a small carton of juice? Get small children into the habit of this and they won't pester for junk food when they go to the cinema.

ANSWER: small portion of salted popcorn

Did you know?

. . . that a fizzy drink concoction at one cinema chain has about 1,700 calories and 100g of sugar? That's about four level tablespoons and more than the official 85g GDA (Guideline Daily Amount) for children and 90g for women (for men it's 120g).

Nuts OR crisps?

If you're in need of some nibbles in the pub, is it best to choose crisps or nuts? Peanuts would keep you going for longer because they contain more protein and fat, but that comes at nearly twice the calorific price. There are about 300 calories and 25g of fat in a small bag of peanuts, but only 184 calories and 11g of fat in a 35g packet of crisps. If you can go for a lower-fat or baked variety of crisps, you'll cut down significantly on the fat. Of course, nuts and crisps are salty — that's why they sell them in the pub: to make you thirsty so you'll drink more. A bag of crisps contain about 0.4g of salt and peanuts about 0.6g.
ANSWER: crisps

Black OR green olives?

As moreish little snacks go, olives are reasonably healthy, thanks to their high level of healthy monounsaturated fats, plus small amounts of vitamin E and other nutrients. Green olives are less ripe than black ones, and slightly lower in calories and fat. Ten green ones would be about 30 calories, while ten black ones would clock up about 70. If they come in olive oil, the calorie intake increases, and if they're packed in brine, they'll make you thirsty, so ask for a glass of water to go with them.
ANSWER: green

Wine OR gin and tonic?

Most of us know the government's guidelines on the amounts of alcohol we should drink: in the UK the RDA of alcohol for women is two to three units daily, and for men three to four. But how fattening our favourite tipples are has not been made so clear. The number of calories in a drink depends on how much alcohol it contains and that varies according to its strength, whether it's wine, a spirit or beer. So to keep within recommended daily alcohol and calorie amounts, you have to do a bit of maths. One unit of alcohol contains 56 calories. A small glass of red, white or rose wine (175ml) is about two units, so that's around 110 calories. A measure of gin (25ml) with a calorie-free mixer is one unit, so that's 56 calories. Gin contains fewer congeners than red wine, substances produced during fermentation that give some alcoholic drinks a darker colour and are thought to contribute to hangovers.

The alcohol and calories in beer, wine and cider can vary between 1.7 units and about 100 calories for a 330ml bottle of premium lager or beer, to three units and about 170 calories for a pint of regular cider. In drinks with added sugar or cream, like alcopops and some liqueurs, the calorie count soars. So, if you have the self-control to stick to one G&T, that's the best option, calorie- and alcohol-wise.

ANSWER: gin and tonic

EXPERT OPINION

A unit of alcohol refers to how much your liver can process in an hour, so that there is none left in your bloodstream. If you drink a large glass of wine (250ml) containing three units of alcohol, it'll take your body about three hours to process it. 'Everyone should have at least two alcohol-free days a week,' suggests Professor Ian Gilmore, chair of the Alcohol Health Alliance.

Did you know?
. . . that a bottle of wine containing ten units of alcohol contains 560 calories? That's the equivalent of two Mars bars, with 280 calories in a 62g bar.

Tips for Dating

As any single person looking for love knows, often the best way of finding 'the one' is by getting out there and dating until you drop. So, as the singles scene grows it's good to follow a few simple rules to make sure you practise safe dating.

First date: drinks OR dinner?

A survey by the polling organization YouGov suggested that in the UK nearly a third of people used some sort of agency, like the Internet or classified ads, to find a date. There's nothing wrong with it — many happy couples have met, and continue to meet, like

this. Relationship counsellors are unanimous in their advice, though, that when you go on a first date with a stranger, you should avoid going out for a meal: you may feel trapped with someone you don't like or even find sinister. Keep it brief, is their advice. They also suggest that women should meet on territory that is familiar to them — their local pub, for example — so that they don't find themselves isolated in an unknown location, and that they let a friend know where they are and what time they expect to get home.
ANSWER: drinks

Touch OR don't touch?

The idea that women find confident, high-status men more attractive than lower-status blokes is hardly surprising. In evolutionary terms, higher-status men were likely to be better mates, so try your best to be confident, guys. Experiments by French psychologist Nicola Guéguen revealed that men who lightly touched a woman on the arm were more likely to get a positive response to a request for a date or a dance than men who didn't. This is thought to be because we rate 'touchers' as more dominant

than the people they touch. Other experiments have shown that people who want something from others are more likely to get it if they touch them. So, if you find someone attractive, a little brush on the arm may get you a long way. Of course, things may also go very wrong, so proceed with caution.
ANSWER: touch

Condom: sooner OR later?

If you are in the habit of having one-night stands, don't wait until you get started before you bring up the subject of condoms. This is especially important for women because it reassures them and makes it clear to the man that they are in control of the situation. It's easy to get carried away in the heat of the moment, and by then it may be too late. Studies in the UK suggest that those who become infected with sexually transmitted infections (STIs) may be more likely to have unsafe sex or lack the skills and confidence to negotiate safer sex. So, get the condom on before there's any genital contact and before using sex toys. The NHS website suggests establishing a line that you won't cross until you bring up the subject. For

example, say to yourself, 'My zip cannot be undone if I haven't talked about using a condom.'
ANSWER: sooner

Eating Out

I once scoured cookbooks written by top restaurant chefs for healthy recipes to include in a newspaper feature. It was surprisingly hard to find any. Dishes made by professional cooks often taste good because they're full of salt, sugar and fat to give them flavour. The trick to healthy eating out (including at fast-food outlets) is to know how to spot dishes laden with these ingredients and avoid them. But rather than looking at the menu and thinking glumly, 'Oh dear, I can't have this or that', look out for all the things you can say yes to and choose from those.

Below are a few dos and don'ts, plus tips on how to eat healthily at different types of restaurant.

Of course, if you aren't watching your weight or concerned about heart disease, *bon appétit*!

Say yes to . . .

- salad-based starters (ask for the dressing on the side or just some balsamic vinegar)
- smoked salmon
- melon
- clear soup
- grilled meat and fish
- a couple of scoops of vanilla ice cream or fruit sorbet
- crème caramel
- fresh fruit salad

Say no to . . .

- massive portions: even though you've paid for it, you don't have to eat it all
- the bread basket
- portions of butter
- anything with cream in it
- deep-fried anything
- anything *au gratin* — it will contain a lot of fat
- veggie options that sound healthy but are often laden with cream or buttery sauces to make them tasty, like vegetable lasagne or quiches and tartlets
- cheese: in sauces or the big portions that are an alternative to dessert
- little chocs that come with coffee

Chinese OR Indian?

Indian food is rich in healthy pulses, like the lentils in dahl, and in vegetables and lean meat, like chicken. But it can also be laden with ghee, a form of butter that is very high in saturated fat. Breads such as puri are fried so they contain hidden calories, and there's more fat in the cream used in malai and korma dishes.

Chinese food — at least, the kind found in many take-aways and restaurants — also has healthy options like lean meat and vegetable dishes. But quite a lot of it is deep-fried, comes with built-in starchy noodles, and salty, sugary sauces — sweet and sour pork, for example. The flavouring MSG (monosodium glutamate) used in Chinese cuisine has also been thought to cause a range of unpleasant symptoms, including nausea, chest pain and drowsiness, known as 'Chinese Restaurant Syndrome', but many studies have failed to prove it.

It's all down to how wisely you navigate the menus, but if you avoid the oily, creamy Indian options and focus on dahls and vegetables with a little meat or fish and some plain rice (one favourite rice dish, pilau, contains fat), Indian food is the healthier choice. Aim to half fill your plate with

vegetables, and the other half with lean protein, plain rice and very little fat.
ANSWER: Indian

Garlic bread OR bruschetta?

You'd think bruschetta, with its healthy topping of raw tomatoes, onions and herbs, would be the healthier choice, but at one big pizza chain the bruschetta contains 534 calories, compared to the same chain's garlic bread, at 238 calories. The extra calories in the bruschetta probably come from the olive oil used to fry the bread and in the topping. If you aren't watching your weight, bruschetta will have more nutrients than garlic bread, but make sure you share it.
ANSWER: garlic bread

Hummus OR taramasalata?

No contest here. Hummus wins hands down — in moderation. The combination of chickpeas, tahini (made from sesame seeds), olive oil and garlic makes it a much healthier starter than taramasalata. The latter is made from protein-rich cod's roe, but not very much of it, with larger amounts of the oil and breadcrumbs that give it its lovely creamy texture. Both hummus and taramasalata are pretty fattening, with about 230 calories and 23g of fat in a 50g serving of taramasalata, and 160 calories and 14g of fat in the same amount of hummus. I find it hard to tell the difference between reduced-fat hummus and the regular sort, so if you're eating it at home it's worth swapping. Reduced-fat taramasalata is also available, if you just can't resist.

ANSWER: hummus

Salad as a starter OR a main?

A small study in the US observed that diners who ate a filling but low-calorie (100 calories) salad with a light dressing as a starter followed by pasta consumed 12 per cent fewer calories during the meal than those who had no starter. They saved 100 calories in one meal. Over a week, that could mean quite a big reduction so eat your salad first! To keep the calories down, go for simple salads that consist mainly of vegetables like leaves, tomatoes and cucumber. Always ask for your dressing on the side so that you're in charge of how much you add, and try to stick to simple oil and lemon juice or vinegar, or plain balsamic. Pour on creamy, cheesy dressings and you're just adding calories and saturated fat.

ANSWER: starter

Pasta OR pizza?

There's nothing wrong with pasta in itself: it's the creamy sauces, fatty meat, cheese and oil that top it. But pasta can be very healthy, especially if the portion isn't too big, the chef's gone easy on the olive oil and it comes with lots of tomato sauce, vegetables and lean protein. A pasta marinara (with seafood) is a good example, or napoletana (with a simple tomato sauce).

The same can't really be said of pizza: it's mainly starch from the base and fat from the cheese topping. And if you add extra ingredients such as meat the calories and fat pile up. Take Pizza Hut's offerings: according to their website, a regular 11-inch Italian pizza ranges, for example, from 1,020 calories, 15.6g of saturated fat and 3.9g of salt for a simple Margarita, to 1,140 calories, 16.2g of saturated fat and 5.4g of salt for a Meat Feast. That's nearly the entire recommended daily amount for an adult of saturated fat and salt. There's a bigger difference between the pasta options, with salmon pasta bake weighing in at 832 calories, 25.4g of saturated fat and 3.27g of salt, and chilli twists with prawns at 525 calories, with 2.3g of saturated fat and 3.83g of salt.

It's easier to find healthy pasta than pizza. Interestingly, Pizza Hut's website only gives the nutritional information per slice, alongside the number of slices in each pizza, so I've had to do the maths. Funny, that.

ANSWER: pasta

KFC OR McDonald's?

Both outlets have made an effort to introduce healthier items to their menus, like salads, juices, alternative fats for frying and, in KFC's case, grilled instead of deep-fried chicken, and McDonald's now displays the calorie content of all meals on its menus. But if you cross the threshold of either, it's probably not your waistline that's uppermost in your mind but the craving for junk food that many of us get from time to time. So, Big Mac or chicken pieces? According to the KFC website, their original recipe meal package — that's three pieces of chicken, fries and a Pepsi — is 1,100 calories. McDonald's

don't give calories for meal packages on their site, but total up a Big Mac, medium fries and a medium Coke and you get 990 calories. Not much to choose between either meal, though you could cut about 160 calories from the McDonald's option by downsizing the fries and Coke to small portions. Or go for a kid's Happy Meal — grown-ups are allowed to eat them too. With a burger, a small portion of fries and orange juice you'll swallow 600 calories. That's a main meal, mind, not a snack.
ANSWER: McDonald's

Doner OR shish kebab?

You may have been a late-night kebab ingester after an evening drinking on an empty stomach, but a kebab *inspector*? A survey by UK local-authority inspectors of 500 doner kebabs found that, without salad and sauces, the average doner kebab contains 98 per cent of our daily salt allowance of 6g, nearly 1,000 calories and 148 per cent of an adult's daily saturated fat allowance (20g for women, 30g for men). 'But it was late,' I hear you say, 'and I was hungry, and nowhere else was open.' Next time opt for a chicken shish kebab and you're looking at just 300 calories and 7g of fat. Ask for your pitta to be stuffed with salad, add a good dash of chilli, which helps to speed up your digestion, and you've had a pretty healthy pit-stop.

ANSWER: shish kebab

Red OR white wine?

Lots of publicity has been given recently to findings that red wine is positively good for us, while there have been no equivalent findings about white wine. One of the so-called magic ingredients in red wine is resveratrol, a substance that may help combat cardiovascular disease and cancer; it is found in greater concentration in some grapes used in red than those used in white wine — albeit still in very small amounts. But as Dr Stephen Barrett points out on his highly respected website, Quackwatch, a lot of the research into resveratrol has been done on animals in laboratories and not on humans. Despite the good news about red wine, don't let the possible benefits outweigh the risks and start knocking back the Cab Sav. There are risks attached to drinking alcohol, such as addiction and liver disease — and, ironically, cardiovascular disease and cancer.

ANSWER: red

Did you know?

. . . that, according to DEFRA, the UK spent £174
billion on food, drink and catering in 2009, of
which 30 per cent was on eating and drinking outside of the home? During tough economic times,
spending on cheap fast food tends to increase.
That means some hefty profits for a catering trade
that likes to fill us up with cheap booze and fatty,
sugary junk.

Evenings In

You may look forward all day to a quiet evening catching up with the family over a home-cooked meal, getting a few chores out of the way and spending me-time on the things you enjoy, but the reality can be very different. Shopping and cooking become a stressful hassle; bickering over jobs to be done or how much time is spent slumped in front of the TV can turn everyday life into a domestic drama.

Understanding how to cut through confusing consumer choices and prepare quick, simple and nutritious suppers, as well as avoiding arguments and getting household jobs done efficiently, are all achievable. And, as insomniacs will be pleased to hear, so is getting a good night's sleep. Here's how.

Shopping for Food

As food prices continue to rise it's more important now than ever to be economical with your weekly shop. Here are some tips to help you make the most out of your shopping, and keep your choices on the healthy side, too.

Organic OR non-organic?

This is an emotive subject, with the pro-organic camp wielding scary facts about pesticide residues in food getting into our bodies. But recent reviews of the evidence said that there is little difference in the nutritional composition of non-organic and organic foods, and no marked health benefits in the latter. If food-safety issues bother you, you may be interested to hear that most outbreaks of food poisoning are linked to hygiene in production and handling rather than contamination of the foodstuff. The organic camp is more convincing on environmental and animal-welfare grounds: industrial-farming methods

117

expose land and water supplies to chemical pesticides and fertilizers, and animals to drugs and growth hormones. Some shoppers also like to support the major investment of time and money by farmers who go organic.

What puts many shoppers off, though, is the extra cost — although a report by the Organic Trade Board showed that many organic basic foodstuffs, including dairy produce, tea and coffee, bread and corn-flakes, can be cheaper than those produced conventionally. Buying own-brand organic foods from a big supermarket chain, for example, could work out cheaper than standard brands in a smaller shop.

If you would like to buy more organic food but can't afford to do it all of the time, you could consider buying organic basic food-stuffs such as carrots and milk, as they only cost a little more than their non-organic counterparts. Alternatively, why not spend what extra you can manage on premium foods, such as a cut of top-quality organic meat once a week, with enough for leftovers? But if it's cost you're worried about, stick with non-organic.

ANSWER: non-organic

Low-fat OR light?

This is a good example of how food labelling can fox you. To say that a food is 'light' or 'lite', it must be at least 30 per cent lower than standard products in at least one typical food value, such as fat or sugar. The label must explain exactly what has been reduced and by how much: for example, 'light: 30% less fat'. If it's a high-fat product like cheese, even the light version can pack in the calories, and a light version of one brand may contain the same amount of fat or calories as the standard version of another.

'Low' is less confusing. A claim that a food is low in fat may only be made when, in a solid item, the product contains no more than 3g of fat per 100g or 1.5g of fat per 100ml in a liquid. If you can't be bothered to read the 'light' label, go for low. Bear in mind, however, that manufacturers often substitute sugar for fat in order to enhance flavour. Fats are essential in our diet so, if your heart is healthy and you don't need to lose weight, full-fat options are fine.

ANSWER: low

Use by OR best before?

The 'best before' label is there to show shoppers the date by which food is no longer at its best (although it's still safe to eat). The 'use by' label is there to show shoppers the date by which the food becomes unsafe to eat (and it tends to appear more on fresh food). While this is the official line, according to the FSA (Food Standards Agency) only 25 per cent of people take any notice. Most of us tend to use our eyes and noses to see if food is OK to eat — if it's mouldy or smelly it probably goes in the bin. This is definitely not advice, however, just a personal observation.
ANSWER: use by

Did you know?
. . . that, although microwaves use a form of radiation to cook food, it is not powerful enough to do chemical damage to your body? It heats food but does not change its structure. If you've worried that using a microwave is dangerous, relax! Microwave ovens use less energy than conventional electric cookers, and also save time as they work so fast. As they are great for heating leftover food or defrosting portions that have been cooked in advance and frozen, that saves time, too. Because you can use small amounts of fat or water to cook

fish or vegetables, microwaving can be very healthy. Just be careful when you take piping-hot food out not to burn yourself, and make sure it's cooked evenly. This is especially important when feeding children.

Frozen OR chilled?

There's a perception that chilled food is somehow healthier than frozen, but that often has more to do with the way it's packaged and presented than fact. Cartons of food stacked up in a freezer rarely look as appetizing as their chilled counterparts. But chilled ready meals can contain more additives and stabilizers than food that's been preserved by freezing. Fish and peas, for example, are frozen so quickly that they may contain more nutrients and be fresher than their chilled counterparts. Frozen food is often cheaper, too: take bags of delicious summer berries from the freezer and compare them with imported out-of-season strawberries. As frozen food lasts longer, it's less likely to be thrown away because it's gone off before you eat it. According to the campaigning group Love Food Hate Waste, the UK throws away 8.3 million tonnes of food from its homes annually, which costs the average family with children £680 a year, or £56 a month, and has serious environmental implications, too.

Don't turn your nose up at tinned veg and fruit either: sweetcorn, beans, peaches and pears are great store-cupboard staples — but look out for fruit in juice rather than syrup.
ANSWER: frozen

Dinner Time

The evening meal is a great time to catch up with friends and family — and a well-cooked, healthy dinner means you can save on eating out and keep your calorie intake in check.

Eat early OR late?

You may have heard that you're less likely to burn calories if you consume them late at night, so it's best to eat early in the evening. Several trials have shown that this is not true. It's how much you eat overall, not when, that counts. People who eat late might be fatter because they eat more throughout the day. Sleep experts, however, advise that eating a big meal or drinking a lot of alcohol late at night can cause digestive problems and

interfere with sleep.
ANSWER: early

Eat together OR separately?

There's been a lot of hand-wringing recently about the demise of the family meal. Everyone is so busy working or doing their own thing after school that it's impossible to sit down together. Apparently this is damaging our social fabric and our health. Some social scientists have found some evidence to suggest that teenagers who eat fewer family meals are more likely to indulge in bad behaviour, such as drug-taking, smoking and drinking alcohol. There is also some evidence that children who eat regularly with their families consume a healthier diet, and in the UK there is also a correlation between more family meals and better exam performance. It's not always clear from the evidence, though, whether 'family meals' stand for something else, like income or social class.

It's easy to romanticize the idea of everyone sitting down at the table having a lovely home-cooked meal and engaging in interesting and entertaining conversation. But family meals can be hellish if the cook is stressed or everyone ends up arguing. They should also be balanced against the advantages of the activities that compete with them, like sport and music.

But given the competing interests that prevent many families spending time together, it's a good idea to try to eat together harmoniously at least a couple of times a week. There's no need to fret over home cooking: a takeaway or ready meal will do. Family meals are as much about learning good social skills and making the most of opportunities to be together as they are about what you eat.

ANSWER: eat together

Did you know?
... that one of the best guides to eating a balanced meal is the 'eatwell plate'? It's a diagram that shows a plate of food consisting of about a third fresh fruit and/or veg and a third carbohydrates, like bread, potatoes, pasta or rice (preferably wholegrain). The remaining third is made up of equal amounts of protein from meat, fish or pulses and from dairy foods like cheese and yogurt, with just a little room left for food and drink high in fats and sugar. Google 'eatwell plate' and an excellent photographic version comes up that you can print out and stick on the fridge.

Raw OR cooked?

Munching uncooked fruit and vegetables and nibbling nuts may sound 'natural', and therefore healthy, but what about the trendy raw-food diet, whereby no cooked food is allowed? Taken to extremes, one German study concluded, a raw-food diet can be harmful, especially to heart health, because it lacks certain essential nutrients. Raw fruit and veg are very high in raw fibre, which can irritate your gut and cause embarrassing wind. Of course salads and fruit are good for you, and nobody would argue that over-cooked vegetables are either nutritious or delicious, or that a vegetarian diet is unhealthy, but a balance between raw and lightly steamed, boiled and stewed is what to aim for.

If you are watching your weight you don't need to add heaps of sugar to most stewed fruit — try adding a little orange or apple juice instead and experimenting with spices like cinnamon to add flavour. Other raw foodstuffs, like eggs, shellfish or meat, can be harmful if not handled carefully, and are not recommended if you are pregnant.
ANSWER: cooked

Broccoli OR spinach?

Both vegetables top lists of super-healthy foods, but if home cooks had to choose between one or the other, which should it be? Spinach is rich in iron, calcium and folic acid — the latter is essential to a developing foetus — plus plenty of other vitamins and nutrients, but you have to eat a lot of it to get the benefit: 80g of cooked spinach counts as a five-a-day portion. That's about a cereal bowl of raw leaves, or roughly two heaped tablespoons of cooked spinach.

Broccoli needs a little trimming, doesn't shrink when you cook it, is just as nutritious, and two decent-sized florets count as a portion.

It's probably best not to boil either vegetable because water-soluble vitamins will be partly wasted. Instead, steam or stir-fry them for a few minutes. You can try converting broccoli-hating kids by serving it like an ice-cream cone. Take a cooked floret, stalk and all, wedge a carrot stick into it so it looks like a chocolate Flake in an ice cream and let them eat it with their fingers.

ANSWER: broccoli

Did you know?

. . . that the term 'superfood' was coined by US eye doctor Steven Pratt in his 2003 book Super-FoodsRx? The term is a bit of a gimmick — if you ate just these foods your diet would not be very balanced. They are so named because of the extra vitamins and minerals they contain beyond the basic food groups, such as protein, fat and carbo-hydrate. The 'superfoods' are:

beans	pumpkin	tomatoes
blueberries	wild salmon	turkey
broccoli	soy beans	walnuts
oat	spinach	yogurt
oranges	tea	

Tomatoes OR statins?

Cardiovascular disease is now the major cause of death worldwide, and statins help lower high blood cholesterol, a risk factor in heart disease. One brand, Simvastatin, is now the UK's most prescribed drug, with 6 million people taking it every year and a low-dose version available over the counter. While doctors agree that statins can help people who have already had a cardiac event, such as a heart attack, by reducing the possibility of another, the jury is out on whether those who have not had one should take them. In a small amount of users they can have serious side effects.

When newspapers report that lycopene, found in tomatoes (and other red vegetables), is as effective as statins, it sounds like good news. But while high amounts of lycopene can lower cholesterol and blood pressure, no proper trials have been done to compare its effectiveness with statins. That's not to say there's no point in eating tomatoes, raw, cooked and even in ketchup, and of course a healthy diet overall can help reduce the risk of cardiovascular disease.

ANSWER: statins

Sunflower OR olive oil?

Our bodies need dietary fats for energy and to support important bodily functions like cell growth, but some fats are healthier than others. Both sunflower oil and olive oil count as healthier fats as they contain mono- and polyunsaturated fats, and less saturated fat than butter — the type associated with higher cholesterol and an increased risk of heart disease. Calorie-wise, there is nothing to choose between them, but there are some nutritional differences: olive oil is richer in monounsaturated fat, which helps to lower blood cholesterol, and sunflower oil is higher in polyunsaturated fats, which contain essential omega-3 and -6 fatty acids. (For more information on fats please refer to page 189.) Sunflower oil is also rich in vitamin E, which helps prevent cell damage and blood clots and boosts our immune system.

You could, of course, use both. Sunflower oil is better for frying as it has a higher burning point, but olive oil is a good all-rounder — for shallow frying and in salad dressings. If you are going to buy just one type of oil, olive oil is probably the best choice.

ANSWER: olive oil

Did you know?
. . . that Parmesan cheese is high in fat and salt? That's why it's so tasty. But a little goes a long way, and it's high in calcium, containing roughly double the amount as the same weight in Cheddar, but only slightly higher in fat and calories. So sprinkle it on salads and pasta instead of a bigger portion of milder cheese.

Cook with wine OR stock?

Adding a glug or two of wine to the pan may seem like a naughty indulgence but some of the alcohol and calories are burned off in the cooking process. How much is left depends on the temperature and cooking time, and how well the alcohol is mixed into the food. A slowly cooked casserole, like boeuf bourguignon, will end up with less alcohol than crêpes Suzette, which are briefly flambéd in the pan. If you are the kind of cook who likes a glug of alcohol while preparing a meal, you may risk drinking more than you meant to. Of course alcohol adds depth of flavour to food, but so do stock, herbs and spices and dashes of Worcestershire or soy sauce and balsamic vinegar — and they're a lot cheaper. **ANSWER:** stock

Weigh portions OR guess?

A former colleague of mine once lost 2.25kg in a month without dieting, taking more exercise or feeling ravenous. Her secret weapon was a pair of scales on which she weighed her food. This may sound like the obsessive behaviour of a Hollywood diva, but one reason experts think we are collectively getting fatter is a huge increase in portion sizes over the last twenty years, thanks largely to a food industry that plays on our greed by offering us mass-produced processed food packed with cheap carbs and fats that costs little to manufacture. Nutritionist Amanda Ursell points out, for example, that a typical scone used to weigh around 50g and provide 151 calories but that the scones now available in our coffee shops can tip the scale at 190g with a whacking 600 calories. Evolutionary biologists believe we are not programmed to resist abundant food; like our ancestors who hunted and foraged for their sustenance — if it's there, we'll eat it. The difference is that these days it's harder to avoid food than it is to find it.

While lots of manufacturers now helpfully put suggested portion sizes on their packaging, they are usually expressed in grams, and how many of us know exactly how many grams of dried pasta, say, are in an 80g serving? It's only a couple of large handfuls. My colleague — who was not overweight, just curious — was surprised by how much she overestimated suggested portion sizes. It might be worth trying this as an experiment for a few weeks. After a while you will automatically know the 'right' portion size.

ANSWER: weigh portions

Slice of cheesecake OR cheese and biscuits?

When it comes to the end of a meal and you can't choose between pudding and cheese, which wins calorie-wise? A 100g portion of blackcurrant cheesecake from a well-known supermarket has 240 calories, of which most come from sugary carbs and fat, and contains only a small amount of the nutrients, such as protein and calcium, found in cheese.

If you are tempted by cheese and biscuits, a 30g match-box sized serving of Cheddar contains 80–100 calories, depending on the type. It's best to go for lower-fat cheeses such as goat, feta and Brie. A couple of wholegrain crackers, like oatcakes, supply about 100 calories. So, cheese and biscuits amounts to fewer calories than the cheesecake, and better nutritional value, too, because they contain far less sugar, a greater proportion of nutrients, and let's not forget fibre from the crackers. Add a few celery sticks or a handful of grapes and you've got one of your five-a-day portions of fruit and veg.

ANSWER: cheese and biscuits

Did you know?

. . . that if you drink half a bottle of wine with your meal that's about 250 calories? Do this every night and that's 1,750 calories a week — almost like eating an extra day's recommended food intake of 2,000 calories for women.

Satsuma OR banana?

Which is the healthiest of all fruit? Impossible to say: they all provide vitamins, fibre and other important nutrients in different amounts, so the 'rainbow diet', which suggests eating as wide a range as possible of different-coloured foods, has a lot to recommend it. But fruit contains sugar, so it is not calorie-free. Scoff three bananas a day and you've eaten more calories than there are in a ham and tomato sandwich, and fewer nutrients, because a healthy sandwich con-tains a better balance of protein, vitamins and carbohydrates. Based on information from weightlossresources.com, the list below shows the number of calories in each fruit per 100g, which is roughly the weight of one large banana or a medium apple.

satsumas	25.6
strawberries	27.6
melons	29.5

pears	34.7
apples	47.5
kiwis	49
grapes	61.5
oranges	62.1
bananas	95

ANSWER: satsuma

Domestic life

From keeping a tidy home to making sure tensions in the household are kept to a minimum — it's not always easy being in charge. But there are some great ways you can make effective use of your time and still run a tight and happy ship.

Do the housework OR hire someone else to do it?

There are lots of good reasons for doing your own housework. First, it keeps you active. Thirty minutes of changing bed linen mops up about 80 calories, scrubbing floors about 120, vacuuming about 110. So a couple of hours' housework could burn around 400 calories. This kind of mindless manual work can be quite relaxing, especially if it's in contrast to your working day.

On the other hand, if you're tense and exhausted, there is nothing nicer than to come home to a clean, tidy house — if you can afford it. And there are more enjoyable ways of getting active, especially if you exercise out of doors with all the well-researched benefits that being close to nature brings (see Lunch, page 84). Exercise is also more sociable than cleaning — and there is plenty of evidence to suggest that you are more likely to stick at it with someone else around to keep you motivated. Friends and green spaces cost nothing. So, if you can afford it, why not pay the cleaner and take your exercise in a more enjoyable way?
ANSWER: hire someone else to do it

Wash at 30 OR 60 degrees?

Recent 'eco-friendly' campaigns have encouraged people to wash their clothes at 30 instead of 40 degrees to save both energy and money. But what about health and hygiene issues — both for you and your washing machine? If you suffer from allergies such as asthma or infections like threadworms it's advisable to wash bedding, towels, handkerchiefs and underwear at 60 degrees to kill off germs or dust mites and their eggs. Dust mites love damp, warm conditions but die off in sunlight — hang your washing outside to dry. An NHS study of hospital pillows in the UK found that a third of their weight was made up of dust mites, their excretions, dead skin, bacteria and saliva. Although it stopped short of saying sharing pillows spreads infection, it found that synthetic pillows are no healthier than feather ones, as is widely assumed, possibly because the fabric used in the latter is more tightly woven to stop feathers escaping and provides a more effective barrier. Wash or replace pillows (not just pillowcases) frequently — although you may not want to go as far as the Ritz Carlton Hotel in New York, which, according to *The Times*, uses large goose-down pillows that it replaces once a month.

An occasional wash at 70 degrees helps to keep the machine clean and free of residue. Constant low-temperature washes encourage the growth of mould and bacteria in the rubber door seal, which should be wiped from time to time with a gentle cleaning agent or white vinegar solution. The door should always be left ajar to reduce the build-up of mould. Lower-temperature washes are fine day-to-day, but to protect

136

your health and that of your machine, a once-in-a-while hot wash is essential.

ANSWER: 60 degrees (occasionally)

Watch TV OR play a computer game?

Media reports in January 2010 caused a lot of excitement when they claimed that a recent study in the journal *Circulation* had shown that watching TV increases your chance of dying early. But it's sedentary behaviour in general, not specifically TV watching, that is associated with modest elevations in the death rate from heart disease and all other causes. That includes computer games, unless they are the active types you play on a games console. But many experts, including author and game designer Jane McGonigal, argue that video games are positively good for us. They increase optimism, she suggests, by making hard things seem possible, arouse our curiosity, encourage our active involvement and give rise to a sense of awe and wonder. Many are social, and can unite friends and strangers in a common cause. You don't get all that from watching TV. While suffering from a concussive illness caused by a mild brain injury, McGonigal, who has a PhD, even invented a computer game to help her get better. It's called Superbetter, and is used by hundreds of people to help them cope with and recover from illness. (For more about teenagers and computers, see Kids, page 183.)

ANSWER: play a computer game

Did you know?

. . . that if you are trying to break a bad habit, like drinking too much in the evenings or never getting around to tidying up, a clear goal is more likely to work than 'I really will go easy on the wine'? According to Professor Richard Wiseman of the University of Hertfordshire, who has conducted extensive research into breaking habits successfully, there are four things you need to know about setting and achieving goals:

- set an overall goal — e.g. to drink less;
- break it down into small steps — decide which days in the next week are going to be alcohol-free and buy your favourite soft drinks;
- list the benefits of achieving your goal — e.g. losing weight, fewer rows with your partner, saving money; and
- go public — tell a friend or family member, use an online tracker or stick a chart on the wall at work.

Have a row OR bite your tongue?

If you've had a long day and just want to unwind, things that bug you at home can have the opposite effect — partners who use up the last of the milk or don't put the rubbish out; children who drop clothes and schoolbags on the floor. 'Better out than in' is the popular received wisdom when it comes to letting off steam — but in *50 Great Myths of Popular Psychology*, the authors (all of whom are professors of psychology) argue that getting angry makes us angrier, risking an escalating row. Anger, they say, is helpful only when it's accompanied by constructive problem-solving designed to address the source of the anger. It's better to express resentment calmly and assertively: 'I realize you don't do it on purpose, but when you use up the last of something and forget to buy more, it bugs me. How about we keep a shopping list in the kitchen that you add things to when they run out?'
ANSWER: bite your tongue

Did you know?
. . . that if partners or family members are becoming a constant source of irritation, affectionate

writing may help you contain yourself? This technique, studied in experiments by US researchers,
showed that participants who spent twenty minutes writing down why a loved one meant so
much to them boosted their happiness and lowered
their stress levels.

Last Thing

The End of the Day

As bedtime approaches it's time to switch off and give your body a well-earned rest.

Soap and water OR cleanser when washing your face?

There's something wholesome about the idea of just using soap and water on your skin, and while it will do the job of keeping pores clean and preventing spots and infections, it can have a drying effect: soap removes the natural oils from the outer layers of the skin and leaves your face feeling unpleasantly tight. According to the British Association of Dermatologists, washing with soap and water can cause dermatitis, a painful or itchy skin condition in those with dry skin. A basic, cheap cleanser applied with cotton wool will remove make-up and grime and help your skin stay hydrated. If you prefer soap and water, then use a moisturizer to plump up the outer layer of your skin afterwards.
ANSWER: cleanser

Bath at night OR in the morning?

A morning bath can set you up for the day, if you have time, but if it's a good night's sleep you're after, a bath will relax you and help to get your body temperature right for sleep. Scientists believe we fall asleep best in a room heated to 20–24 degrees centigrade, but that during the night we need to cool down and about 17 degrees is best. (That's why you keep waking up if you get too hot.) Having a hot bath may seem counter intuitive, but it actually helps the cooling-down process because our core body temperature drops rapidly once we're out of the bath. A nice hot bath an hour or so before bed seems to be the best time.

ANSWER: at night

Did you know?
. . . that if you're feeling lonely a hot bath might cheer you up? Research at Yale University suggests that people who feel lonely take baths and showers more frequently, and at hotter temperatures. The reasons are not clear, but it may be because physical warmth is comforting: it is associated with closeness to others and helps reduce the sense of social isolation.

Food diary OR list of good things?

Nutritionists often recommend that dieters keep a food diary, listing daily everything they have eaten. It helps them to stop kidding themselves that they have eaten less than they really have. But even that isn't foolproof: food diaries are notoriously inaccurate, with hundreds of calories sometimes mysteriously unaccounted for. If you are on a diet, however, and finding it hard to stay motivated, there is now a lot of evidence to show that writing down positive thoughts, events or feelings makes us feel happier, whether it's the things we're grateful for or imaginary descriptions of a happy future. Unless you are able to write, 'Hooray, lost half a kilo', a list of good things may not make you thinner, but perhaps you'll feel happier about yourself and more positive about sticking to the diet.

ANSWER: a list of good things

Have sex OR go to sleep?

Couples who are busy juggling jobs with raising children often find that they simply don't have enough time or energy left for sex, and may stop having it altogether. But lack of lovemaking, especially in long-term relation-ships, is associated with depression and psychological problems: couples who don't have sex also have more arguments, feel stressed and worthless, and their self-esteem is low. Inevitably, a sexual desert is associated with increased risk of divorce and relationship dissolution.

Research by Rosemary Besson, an expert on female sexual desire, suggests that the way to overcome this, especially for women, is to get on with it — sex, that is. In interviews with hundreds of women, she discovered that desire is not the *cause* of lovemaking but, rather, its *result*. This is because, while women may not feel desire at the start of sex, as things get going they become aroused and desire follows. Men, on the other hand, are more likely to get aroused by the *idea* of lovemaking, which is why pornography, partners dressing up in sexy undies or suggestive sweet talk can turn them on.

ANSWER: have sex

Insomnia: stay in bed OR get up?

In our 24/7 culture people worry that we are becoming sleep deprived. However, sleep scientists, like Emeritus Professor Jim Horne of the University of Loughborough Sleep Research Centre in the UK, are sceptical about this, arguing that studies show that adults need only seven to seven and a half hours' sleep a night, with an absolute minimum of about five hours. Our bodies are able to adjust to varying amounts of sleep: before electric light, our ancestors slept longer during the winter than in summer, especially in areas where there were big seasonal differences in daylight hours, so we're all able to cope with the odd night of bad sleep.

Insomnia takes many different forms, but typically it includes difficulty in getting off to sleep, and/or waking frequently during the night or very early in the morning, unable to drop off again. If this gets too much, specialist doctors recommend a short course of tablets, usually a form of tranquillizer, combined with cognitive behavioural therapy to address the underlying psychological cause. Unless there is a medical reason for sleep problems, they are very often due to anxiety — the stuff that 'keeps you awake at night' — exacerbated by another typical trait of insomniacs: worrying about their insomnia. That's why relaxing pills with therapy are effective.

The basic message seems to be that, if you

find yourself unable to get off or back to sleep on a regular basis, worrying about it makes it worse.

For this reason it's best to try to distract yourself with something that will focus your attention but not over stimulate your brain — counting sheep, deep breaths in and out, or taking an imaginary walk around a beautiful garden and looking at the flowers in detail. If that doesn't work, your best bet is to get up and try doing something mindless and repetitive such as a jigsaw or some ironing. Still awake? See your doctor.

ANSWER: get up

Did you know?

. . . that although snoring is a subject for jokes, sleeping with a snorer is anything but? There are several causes of snoring and several potential remedies. The British Snoring and Sleep Apnoea Society has a series of tests on its website: britishsnoring.co.uk, which snorers can do at home to find out what type they are, then try the suggested remedies. These range from mechanical gadgets, such as the slightly scary-sounding 'mandibular advancement devices' (which adjust the position of the jaw in order to open up the airway), to drops and sprays, changes in bedding and possible surgery. As the partner of a snorer, I have

148

resorted to wearing foam ear-plugs, available from any pharmacy, which muffle the noise. (They are also useful on overnight flights.) I try to make sure I drop off to sleep before my husband.

Snorers who stop breathing for more than ten seconds more than ten times every hour may be suffering from sleep apnoea; they wake up with a very loud snort — the brain's way of making sure it continues to get some air. The condition can have possible serious health consequences because it deprives the body not just of sleep but also of oxygen. If you think you may have it, see a doctor: a minor operation may fix it.

Weekends

Sometimes weekends can be a terrible let-down. You look forward to them all week only to find yourself looking forward to going back to work on Monday morning. Maybe your willpower deserted you and you woke up with a terrible hangover, blew your plans to eat better or your intentions to exercise, or maxed out on your credit card yet again. Perhaps family tensions created a bad atmosphere. Or were you simply overwhelmed by piles of dirty washing and household errands? If you live alone, it's easy to fall into a trap of thinking that everyone else is having all the fun and wonder where you went wrong. There's definitely an art to making the most of the weekend, and this section is full of tips to help you do so.

Treat Yourself

It's the weekend — time to enjoy your free time and indulge yourself. Make sure to choose the right treats and then you really can make the most of your two days off work.

Sleep late OR get up?

Tempting as it is, sleeping in for several hours at the weekend will disrupt your regular sleep pattern and make it harder to get up early on Monday morning. You are more likely to feel refreshed and relaxed by spending time doing something you really enjoy during the day or getting some exercise. If you do sleep late, you might notice your dreams more: the type of sleep during which we dream lengthens as the night wears on.
ANSWER: get up

Did you know?
. . . that if you wake up with a hangover headache it's probably caused by dehydration? The effects of

excess alcohol on your body include dilated blood vessels in your head, causing a headache; dehydration; nausea due to an irritated stomach lining; and low blood sugar. Take a painkiller, such as ibuprofen or paracetamol, and drink as much fluid as you can get. Water is best as it's least likely to irritate an upset stomach, but any non-alcoholic liquid will do. And as soon as you can manage it, eat something nourishing but easy to digest, like a lean bacon sandwich or toast and peanut butter.

Did you know?

. . . that you are probably either an owl or a lark? We all have an internal body clock located in our brain but in some people it ticks faster and they have more energy early in the day — the larks. Others have slower clocks and are still going strong late at night — the owls. Of course there are variations within each type, and environmental factors affect our sleeping patterns, too, but sleep scientists believe there is a genetic component in whether we are owls or larks. So there isn't much point in forcing yourself to get up earlier or go to bed later than you feel is natural. If you have had a series of very late nights, or there's a long day ahead, it's definitely worth trying to get in an early night as our bodies can pay off a 'sleep debt' and also 'store' sleep.

Cooked breakfast OR continental?

If you enjoy eggs, bacon and all the trimmings at the weekend, you might feel guilty as fry-ups have a bad reputation. It's the fatty foods, like sausages, black pudding and fried bread, that cause the problems, plus, of course, the frying. Continental breakfasts may sound light, but if you go for croissants or baguette with butter and jam, and milky coffee, that's hardly a guilt-free option either. There are about 300 calories in a large plain croissant — and nearly all of them come from saturated fat and refined carbohydrate. A traditional cooked breakfast with a slice of lean back-bacon, some tomatoes, mushrooms — grilled, not fried — and a poached egg on wholegrain toast will come in at about the same, provide you with more sustaining protein, less fat and two of your daily fruit and veg portions. Enjoy!
ANSWER: cooked breakfast

Sunday roast OR bread and cheese?

The Sunday roast is another tradition with a bad nutritional reputation. Of course, if the meat is fatty and you load your plate with roast potatoes, buttered vegetables, gravy made with fat from the meat, plus a dollop of sugary mint or cranberry sauce, it's not the healthiest option. But a couple of slices of roast chicken or turkey (no skin — that's where most of the fat lives) and lots of different vegetables, two medium roast potatoes and fat-free gravy is a different story. You can make the gravy healthier by pouring off the fat from the roasting pan, adding a little of the vegetable cooking water, plus some seasoning, stirring and scraping the bottom of the pan to deglaze it, then boiling the liquid to thicken it. Add any juices from the plate you carve the meat on, plus extra vegetable water if you need to. The whole meal will come in at about 500 calories.

While there's nothing wrong with bread, cheese, a little salad and some pickle, a large wedge of Cheddar and a hunk of crusty white bread is more like a 1,000 calories, with lots of saturated fat and refined carbohydrate. Brie is a better option, as it has about three-quarters of the calories of Cheddar, many of which are just beneath the rind, so cut it off. Wholegrain bread is more nutritious and will keep you going for longer.

ANSWER: Sunday roast

Did you know?

. . . that, according to sleep expert Professor Jim Horne, a cup of coffee before a twenty-minute nap promotes refreshing sleep? Any longer and you risk going into deep sleep, which will leave you feeling groggy and may interfere with that night's sleep. The coffee will take about twenty minutes to kick in so you'll feel alert when you wake up. The best time to snooze, experts suggest, is between about 1 and 3 p.m., during the post-lunch slump.

Ice cream OR an ice pop?

Almost irresistible on a lovely summer's day, but if you're in doubt as to which to choose, ice pops are lower in calories. They're full of sugar, of course, and the slower you suck, the worse for your teeth — and they contain all sorts of additives — but this is a treat after all, and ice pops tend to be lower in fat than ice cream. One popular brand of ice pop, for example, contains about ninety calories and almost no fat. Fruit lolly and ice cream combinations contain about the same amount of calories, but more fat. A 100ml serving of vanilla ice cream will have about 100 calories, with the cone adding about 20–50 extra calories, depending on the type, while a standard Magnum is more like 275. Websites like loveicecream.com are a good source of information, or just read the label if you want to find out the real ice pop lowdown. Healthier ice pops are easy to make by freezing juice or yogurt in moulds available from cookshops or online.

ANSWER: ice pop

Shopping

We spend all week earning our crust so there's nothing like a bit of retail therapy at the weekend to make those hours spent toiling at work seem worthwhile. But shop wisely — you can make your money go much further.

Buy something OR do something?

Research has shown that when people were asked to compare how good they felt about an object they had bought and a recent enjoyable experience, both had cheered them up but the experience won hands down. We tend to preserve happy memories of experiences like a weekend away, forgetting about the terrible traffic jam en route; objects become tatty or break. Also, we are more likely to share experiences with others, adding a positive social dimension. So, if it's a choice between buying a new CD or going to a concert, go to the concert.

ANSWER: do something

Shop online OR in-store?

While online shopping is on the rise and high street spending is declining, interesting psychological factors lie behind our motivation in doing either. A survey of food shoppers in May 2011, by leading research company ESA, found that they were more aware of offers in-store than online, but that many preferred shopping online because they would avoid temptation.

A 2010 laboratory study by the California Institute of Technology suggested we value things more highly when we can touch the real object than when we look at an image of it or read a description. So, to avoid carrying home bags of shopping loaded with three-for-the-price-of-two offers, or splurging on the gorgeous, silky number you can't afford, it's best to stay indoors.

ANSWER: shop online

Pay by cash OR credit card?

Our brains find it difficult to balance the conflict between paying for something later that brings us pleasure instantly. 'I want it now,' they tell us, 'never mind the consequences.' Neuroscientists, like Jonah Lehrer, believe that the parts of our brain that deal with emotional satisfaction and rational thinking come into conflict when making decisions about buying something on credit that we know we can't really afford. If the emotional part wins, we may spend a lot more by paying with a credit card than with cash — that's why shops encourage us to use them by plying us with store cards. Neuroscientists also suggest that when we use credit cards our brains are less likely to register negative feelings than when we part with a big wad of money — wallets that literally feel lighter are more likely to bring the message home than a credit-card receipt. A study by researchers at MIT also demonstrated that people's willingness to pay for goods is increased when they are instructed to use a credit card rather than cash. Their conclusion? Always leave your credit card at home.
ANSWER: cash

Treat yourself OR someone else?

Some of us find shopping so comforting that it becomes 'retail therapy', and studies have shown that people may spend more if they're feeling down. If this becomes a habit it can be very destructive, leading to debt and relationship problems. Researchers think that shopping can become addictive in the same way as gambling or smoking because the habit feeds the parts of our brain that deal with rewards and satisfaction, which then demand more feeding. Hence the not-so-funny 'shopaholic' label.

While it seems that buying a little treat may cheer you up, you may end up feeling more pleased with your purchase if it's for someone else: several experiments have shown that people who spend money on others feel happier than when they spend it on themselves. Neuroscientists believe that the parts of our brain that deal with meeting our basic needs also deal with helping others. Feeling good about buying someone a present may relate back to our primitive ancestors needing to survive in groups.

ANSWER: treat someone else

Did you know?

. . . that a good way to avoid coming home from shopping without the crucial items you set out to buy is to keep a running shopping list? Have a pad in the kitchen and write on it the things you need as you run out of them. You can train flatmates or family to cooperate (be prepared for children to write 'sweets, ice cream, crisps, fizzy drinks . . . ').

Get Active

Weekends are also a time when you catch up on the domestic chores you've been steadfastly ignoring all week. However, if you focus on tackling the big jobs — especially the ones that bring you out in a sweat — you can tick your exercise routine off your list too.

Multitask OR do one thing at a time?

If you find yourself running around like the proverbial headless chicken at weekends, trying to catch up on lots of chores and errands, perhaps you've fallen for the myth of multitasking — that being able to chop and change between different tasks is a great way to get things done. Brain scientists, including Exeter University's Stephen Monsell and

Sophie Leroy of the University of Minnesota, call this process task switching. Their research suggests that when we switch between different tasks it takes us *longer* to complete each one. If we complete a task, it is less likely to interfere with our doing the next one: we have ticked it off mentally and it doesn't niggle at us when we move on. People who multitask effectively are usually practised at what they're doing — that's why you can drive along a familiar route while singing along to songs on the radio.

ANSWER: one thing at a time

Clean the windows OR the car?

There's something a bit depressing about grimy windows that spoil a lovely view or reduce the amount of sunlight indoors. A dirty, messy car that's full of bits of paper, covered in pet hairs and bits of congealed food can be dispiriting, too. Routine cleaning jobs can be very satisfying and are good exercise, but cleaning the windows burns fewer calories than cleaning the car inside and out — around 160 and 200 an hour respectively — because those who clean their cars are likely to do more all-round bending and stretching. A word of warning about cleaning windows: most deaths and serious injuries caused by DIY jobs at home involve falls from ladders, often when people overreach instead of moving the ladder. So, if you do clean the windows, make sure the ladder is firm on the ground and at a stable angle.

ANSWER: clean the car

Vacuum the floor OR mow the lawn?

Of course, both will make you feel virtuous, but there are lots of reasons why pushing a mower around (and a spot of other gardening) might be better for you. It burns more calories, about 190 in thirty minutes as opposed to 110 for vacuuming. And although many studies now back up the idea, you don't have to be a psychologist to know that being outside and close to nature can lift your mood.

ANSWER: mow the lawn

All your exercise now OR break it up?

It may seem a good idea to get in one long exercise session at the weekend if you're busy during the week, and of course this is better than nothing. However, expert advice points to aiming, ideally, for about 150 minutes a week, broken up into three slots, which can include not only sporting activities but also mowing the lawn and a brisk walk or cycle to work. Five sessions of thirty minutes each is fine, otherwise two seventy-five-minute sessions of something strenuous like rugby or heavy digging will suffice. The key is to raise your heart rate and feel a little bit out of breath and sweaty.

If the weekends are the only time that you can get really active, what type of exercise is best? Something you enjoy, is probably the most important consideration. It's hard to stick at something you dislike. But factors such as your weight, fitness level, whether you are more likely to stick at it in a group or on your own all come into play, and if you suffer from heart or breathing problems you should consult your doctor first. Warming up and down exercises, such as stretching calf muscles and hamstrings, are particularly important to avoid injury — the more out of condition you are, the more likely this is to occur. Middle-aged men who decide it's time to start playing football at the weekend after years of inactivity are more likely to end up with a knee injury than as top scorer for their team.
ANSWER: break it up

Run on the flat OR uphill?

If running is your favourite way of keeping fit, leading fitness trainer Matt Roberts suggests finding a grassy slope in a park or the countryside and alternating running up it briskly for a minute with running down more slowly for two minutes in a zig-zag motion, rather than running in a straight line. It's a great way to increase you heart health and metabolic rate — the speed at which your body burns up calories. The technical term for this type of activity is 'interval training'. You can get the same benefits by sprinting for a minute and jogging for two on the flat but it's probably easier and more fun to let Mother Nature give you a helping hand. Beginners should aim for six repetitions, intermediates eight and the fighting fit can go for ten. If you feel faint at the thought of this, team games like baseball or Frisbee, which you can play in the park or on the beach, involve short, sharp bursts of activity, combined with periods of rest, although it's not always easy to get a group together on a regular basis.

ANSWER: run uphill

Run barefoot OR in trainers?

Running with no shoes on may sound like torture, and it's not necessarily an easy option for many city-dwelling folk, but it's what our ancestors did for millennia. Now it's increasing in popularity, thanks to the theory, backed up by research at Harvard University, that running in trainers is bad for the feet. Supportive footwear masks the impact of striking the ground hard, which sends potentially damaging shock waves through the joints, causing painful conditions such as shin splints. The theory goes that, as it's too painful to land on the heel with bare feet, barefoot runners put more weight on the balls of their feet with slightly bent legs and tread more carefully. One barefoot runner I know says she loves the way she treads more lightly — but she always runs on a soft surface, like turf, never on tarmac, and she must have a fairly good eye for spotting hazards like broken glass and dog poo. There's no hard scientific evidence to support one type of running over another, but if you're a novice it would be advisable to go on a course first — see naturalrunning.co.uk. If you do wear trainers it's well worth going to a specialist running shop to get advice on

what type will best suit your needs.
ANSWER: trainers

Arnica OR an ice pack?

Arnica is thought to reduce swelling, bruising and pain but, although it was the first homeopathic medicine to be licensed in the UK by the Medical and Healthcare Products Regulatory Agency (MHRA), there is no sound scientific evidence that arnica is effective. It is available as pills, and as a cream for treating bruising, which is caused by bleeding in underlying tissues. However, ice is an effective remedy as it can reduce bleeding, muscle spasm and pain; it will also prevent swelling and numbness. For the first forty-eight to seventy-two hours after the injury, apply ice wrapped in a damp towel to the injured area for fifteen to twenty minutes every two to three hours during the day. Don't leave it on while you're asleep or let the ice touch your skin directly: it may cause a cold burn. Marathon runners, like Paula Radcliffe and the comedian Eddie Izzard, often submerge themselves in ice baths to reduce inflammation and swelling. A bag of frozen peas will do for lesser mortals.
ANSWER: ice pack

Sports/energy OR juice drink?

It's common sense that if you're losing bodily fluid by exercising hard, especially on a hot day, you need to top up. But so-called sports and energy drinks are often packed with sugar and caffeine, so read the label before you buy. Half a litre of a popular brand of energy drink, for example, contains 140 calories and some caffeine. The equivalent quantity of a popular sports drink contains 135 calories but no caffeine. It's inadvisable to give children caffeinated drinks, and you can make your own cheap, healthy version of an energy-boosting drink by mixing two parts water with one part fruit juice; if you are exercising for long periods of time, a tiny pinch of salt will replace what you lose in sweat.

ANSWER: juice drink

Regret OR let it go?

Weekends can often seem endless, especially if you live alone. Without the distraction of work, there is plenty of time to brood on what's not right with your life. Regrets can be useful: they may help you work out what's important to you. Instead of regarding them

as negative, use them to determine your future. If you regret not having taken a job you were offered, ask yourself what about that job was important to you. What do you feel you missed out on? From there you can work out your values and what you want from your life. It's usually making the 'wrong' decisions or none at all that causes us to regret. In the future, do your research, trust your intuition and accept that no decision is 'wrong': it's just a way of learning what you want.
ANSWER: let it go

Kids

Raising a family, especially if you're trying to hold down a busy job, is extremely demanding. Trying to cram in so-called quality time with everyone while keeping on top of domestic duties and your own personal needs can leave you feeling utterly drained, while parenting advice is so full of conflicting opinions that it can be bewildering. Here are ten basic tried-and-tested suggestions based on expert opinion and my own experience as a full-time working mother.

Babies and Young Children

Keeping children happy without giving in to endless pestering, and resisting feelings of inadequacy because you're not the perfect parent, can help you stay on top of things.

Homemade OR ready-made baby food?

Of course you know you should be puréeing lots of nutritious homemade food for your little ones and putting spare portions in the freezer ready for the week ahead, but in busy working households that can be a tall order. You may prefer to spend your time off actually playing with your baby rather than chopping organic vegetables and fiddling with freezer bags.

Commercially produced baby foods are still viewed with suspicion in some quarters, but in the UK the composition of manufactured foods for children under the age of one is tightly regulated. All artificial colours, preservatives and sweeteners are banned; sugar and salt levels must be kept to a minimum. Use of pesticides is also tightly controlled. True, the food loses some of its vitamins in the heat treatment it undergoes to kill bacteria and give it a long shelf life, but this does not affect other nutrients.

For children over the age of one, the rules relax: read the labels carefully and make sure you are happy with the ingredients. Look out for added sugar, salt, additives and high saturated-fat levels.

ANSWER: ready-made (when necessary)

Leave babies to cry OR comfort them?

This is a highly contentious and emotive issue, but one of the biggest adjustments that many new parents have to deal with is disrupted sleep. If you're not working and can sleep during the day when your baby does, it's not so hard to cope with one who sleeps irregularly at night. If you have to go to work, though, it can be very debilitating.

Some experts say that it may be harmful in the long run to leave babies to cry as their brains may be exposed to high levels of stress hormones. But others, like Professor Tanya Byron in an article in *The Times* in October

2010, point out that the studies backing this argument have been done in negative environments, such as orphanages.

It would be very distressing for everyone to leave a baby to cry for hours on end, but some parents cannot bear to hear their babies cry at all and prefer to comfort them straight away. Others use controlled crying — letting the baby cry and gradually extending the period before picking it up, and camping out — reassuring the baby without picking it up. A September 2012 study in the journal *Pediatrics* suggested that eight-month-old babies whose parents found these techniques reduce sleeping problems had come to no harm when followed up five years later. Those who struggle on, giving attention to their children as soon as they demand it, often end up with 'little emperors' who rule the roost.

My mother's advice was to leave a baby to cry for about twenty minutes maximum at bedtime and train yourself to hear the difference between grizzling and loud, distressed crying, which indicates that something is wrong. I followed her advice, and that of friends who told me that routine in the evenings is very important — food, bath, stories, songs, bed. Always. Both my children slept through the night from about eight weeks: from a late feed at about 11 p.m.

until about 5 in the morning.

ANSWER: leave babies to cry (for short periods)

Baby in bed OR in a cot?

Like picking up a crying baby, this is another contentious and emotive issue. The advice from the Department of Health and the Foundation for the Study of Infant Deaths is that babies should sleep in a cot in their parents' room, for the first six months, unless the parents smoke in the room, in which case the baby should sleep somewhere else. Babies should be put to sleep on their backs to reduce the risk of cot death and their feet should be at the bottom of the cot with the blankets tucked in no higher than their shoulders. The danger of having your baby in bed with you is that it may be smothered by your bedding, or too hot, which also increases the risk of cot death. Official recommendations also advise against sharing a bed with your baby if you have been drinking or taking drugs.

While snuggling up in bed at night, especially if you're breastfeeding, is wonderfully cosy, and very tempting if you're exhausted and getting up several times a night to feed, it will be a hard habit for your baby to break and you may find you're driving, literally, an ever-larger wedge between you and your partner that can cause relationship difficulties.

ANSWER: in a cot

Did you know?

. . . that there is no legal age in the UK at which children — i.e. young persons under the age of eighteen — may be left at home alone? It's up to the parents' discretion. But parents can be prosecuted for neglect if they put their children at risk of injury or suffering. If you leave your children with a babysitter who's under the age of sixteen, they are not legally responsible for what happens to your children — you are. Whoever you leave your child with, always have an agreed plan for emergencies in place.

Use a straw OR sip drinks?

Because the sugar and acids in fruit juice and fizzy drinks are bad for children's teeth (yours, too), dentists recommend giving them at mealtimes only and using a straw once they're old enough so that the drink makes less contact with their teeth.

ANSWER: use a straw

Milkshake OR ice cream?

The word 'milk' makes anything sound wholesome, but if it's a choice between a commercially produced milkshake and a couple of scoops of ice cream, the latter is usually healthier. It's hard to be sure what's gone into a milkshake, apart from the milk, but it's likely to be sugary syrup. Milkshakes also tend to come in large serving sizes, whereas you can always just ask for one scoop of ice cream. One US milkshake with chocolate ice cream and peanut butter was reported recently to contain 2,000 calories, and the same amount of saturated fat as twenty-five rashers of bacon. Although contents will vary hugely from one manufacturer to another, at McDonald's, for example, a reduced-fat vanilla cone has 150 calories while a small vanilla milkshake has 220. You can make your own delicious, healthier versions at home with a hand blender using milk, soft fruit, like banana or strawberry, and a few drops of vanilla extract.
ANSWER: ice cream

Did you know?

. . . that there is little scientific evidence to back up the theory that giving children sugar provokes a 'sugar high'? If you've ever arrived to pick yours up from a party and found them rampaging around, you've probably seen other parents rolling their eyes and heard them blaming sugar. While the sugar in party foods, such as cake, biscuits and sweet drinks, does give an energy boost, it could be that children get overexcited by the party itself, and that parents perceive their children (and especially other people's) to be 'hyper' when they're not. A possible explanation for the sugar-high/low idea is that refined sugars and carbohydrates, such as are found in party food, are absorbed into the bloodstream quickly and can trigger fluctuating blood-sugar levels. This may also increase production of adrenalin, which makes children more active. When it drops they may slow down again.

One sport OR lots?

While all children need plenty of exercise to let off steam, keep fit and maintain an appropriate weight, some parents dream of their offspring becoming a future striker or Wimbledon champion. Should children focus on one activity or try lots?

UK government guidelines recommend

that children under five who can walk unaided should be physically active every day for at least 180 minutes (three hours), spread throughout the day, indoors or out. They need to get a bit 'puffed out' through plenty of activities like running around, riding bikes and dancing. Children and young people aged five to eighteen should do at least sixty minutes of activity daily that raises their heart rate, such as fast walking or playing in the playground, running or karate, every day. They also need to do muscle-strengthening activities, such as gymnastics and hanging off playground bars, and bone-strengthening activities such as skipping and playing football.
ANSWER: lots

Did you know?

. . . that it's perfectly OK for children to watch TV? There are plenty of fun and interesting programmes for them, and cuddling up on the sofa to watch a DVD or TV series everyone enjoys is a relaxing way to spend family time. However, there's growing evidence to indicate that too much TV is a bad thing. Hours spent sitting in front of the TV raises the risk of childhood obesity, and watching it late at night, especially in a teenage bedroom long after parents have gone to sleep, can interfere with regular sleeping patterns. Children who are allowed to constantly flick between one channel and the next can experience difficulties in concentrating. As with playing computer games, parents can tame the TV monster by setting the rules (you are in charge) about what and when their children can watch. When they are old enough, let them look at the TV schedules and work out between you what they can watch. The same idea applies to computer games.

Teenagers

Living with teenagers isn't always easy, but giving them a little leeway here and there should lead to a happier home life.

Alcohol OR soft drinks for teenagers?

In some countries it's legal to give alcohol under supervision to children at home from the age of five, and some parents argue that this is a good way to introduce them to sensible drinking. This may be wishful thinking: studies show that it has the opposite effect, and doctors are concerned that children introduced to alcohol at drunken family occasions may go on to indulge in adult binge-drinking sessions. Teenage brains are still developing and scientific evidence links alcohol in child-hood to a range of physical- and mental-health problems, including liver and brain damage, poor memory and reduced growth. Every year in the UK, for example, about 7,500 children between eleven and seventeen are admitted to hospital because of alcohol. In the US, where research has found a negative association between academic achievement and alcohol, the legal drinking age is twenty-one.

Of course, the more you forbid teenagers to do something, the more likely they are to do it in secret, but if your teenagers are drinking, they should understand how much alcohol their drinks contain and know the recommended number of daily units (three to four for a man, two to three for a woman). Alcopops, cynically targeted at young people by the drinks industry, have about 1.5 units in a small bottle. There are up to three in a pint of beer or cider, more if it's premium strength. A 25ml measure of vodka or other spirit is one unit. Experts suggest that family meals are the best time to allow teenagers to drink because the food slows down the absorption of alcohol and the setting allows sensible discussion of the subject.

ANSWER: alcohol under supervision

Computer/TV in the bedroom OR living room?

Parents who have discovered their children texting well into the small hours or falling asleep listening to an iPod will not be surprised to hear that a recent survey of twelve-to-sixteen-year-olds found that 98 per cent of them said they had some sort of electronic gadget in their bedroom. If true, experts are concerned that this means they are not getting the recommended eight to ten hours' sleep, with detrimental effects on their health, and their ability to concentrate at school. Sleep-deprived children tend to be overweight because they crave starchy foods to give them an energy boost during the day. Some scientists, such as Professor Susan Greenfield of Oxford University, also believe, controversially, that the way young people consume digital media, constantly switching between one source of information or entertainment and another, may affect the way their developing brains are wired. Possible consequences could be poorer communication skills and an inability to think in abstract terms.

While the actual risk of 'stranger danger' is very small, the Internet, despite all its undeniable attractions and advantages, enables children to access subject matter and individuals that parents feel should have no part in their lives — that is probably what parents worry about most. Now that smartphones let kids go online wherever and whenever they like, it's harder to keep track, but it's easier if some gadgets are in a shared family space. At least you will have some idea of what they're accessing and for how long. It is more constructive to agree on some ground rules about computer time and make sure they are stuck to than to institute an outright ban or pull out the plug in desperation. In our house 'No Gadget Sunday' is a weekly respite from iPads, DSs and other digital media, apart from bona-fide Internet access for homework, and TV programmes or DVDs that we try to watch together.

ANSWER: in the living room

Teenagers: sleep late OR get up?

If you're busy catching up with weekend errands and chores it can be irritating to know that your teenager is still fast asleep upstairs at lunchtime. But neuroscientists, like Professor Russell Foster of Oxford University, believe that teenagers' body clocks run behind those of children and adults and that they naturally go to sleep and wake up later. Tests have also suggested that they are more alert later in the day than earlier. Waking them early means they are in a state akin to permanent jetlag, says Professor Foster — something most parents of adolescents will recognize. One English secondary school has even delayed the start of the school day until 10 a.m. to allow for this, according to *The Times*. It claims improved attendance and a big hike in GCSE scores as a result.

ANSWER: sleep late

And Finally . . .

Say yes OR no?

Anyone who looks after children of whatever age will feel the emotional battle scars of always having to say no to endless requests for crisps, sweets, fizzy drinks, trips to the cinema, fast-food outlets or time in front of the computer and TV. Once in a while it's fun to have a 'yes' day, when you say yes to pretty much everything. Holidays, birthdays or other special occasions are a good time to do this. The children will be delighted and, while they will certainly make outlandish and extravagant requests, getting the hang of the idea that you can't say yes to absolutely all of them becomes part of the fun.

ANSWER: say yes (once in a while)

The Lowdown on Nutritional Information

If you're watching your weight or trying to cut back on certain types of fat, added sugars and salt — which lead to problems like heart disease, diabetes and cancer if we eat too much of them — there's no substitute for reading labels. However, while nearly all packaging now gives information about the contents, it's often a bit confusing. The red, orange and green traffic light labels are the easiest to understand, but many food companies and supermarkets have resisted using them, because they don't want products with red warning symbols on their shelves. No surprise there.

In order to help you navigate your way around food labels, the following chapter gives you some basic facts to help you understand what to really look out for.

Guideline Daily Amounts (GDAs)

GDAs are the official suggestions for how much of a certain food type or nutrient a healthy, average-sized adult or child should consume per day. The following table gives you the low-down on the basics:

Typical Values	Women	Men	Children
— kcal (Calories)	2000	2500	1800
Protein	45g	55g	24g
Fat	70g	95g	70g
of which saturates	20g	30g	20g
Fibre	24g	124g	15g
Sodium*	2.4g	2.4g	1.4g
*Equivalent as salt	6g	6g	4g

The Lowdown on Fats

- A gram of any type of fat contains 9 calories. That's about double the amount found in protein and carbohydrates. While fats help you to feel full, cutting down on your fat intake is an effective way to lose weight.

189

- High-fat foods include cheese, butter, red meat, pies, cakes and confectionery.

- Our bodies need dietary fat: it is of key importance in cell and hormone production. The GDA for fat intake is 70g for women and children and 95g for men. But some fats are thought to be more helpful than others.

- Monounsaturated fats are found in different food groups, notably olive and rapeseed oils; they are good for heart health and helping to regulate blood-sugar levels.

- Polyunsaturated fats are found mainly in plant-based foods and, like monounsaturated fats, are beneficial to heart health.

- Saturated fats come mainly from animals; while they are essential for our bodies, in high amounts they may raise blood cholesterol levels, which in turn can increase the risk of heart disease. Saturated fat is also found in palm oil, which is used often in processed food, and in coconut oil, which is used in Asian and Caribbean cooking. The recommended daily intake of saturated fat is 30g for men and 20g for women. A medium pork pie (300g) contains about 30g of saturated fat, and a packet of chocolate buttons (32g) about 20g of saturated fat.

- There are concerns that trans fats are more damaging than saturated fats. Trans fats are found in small quantities in animal fats, but we consume most of them in processed foods like biscuits and cakes; they are a by-product of 'hydrogenation', a process that turns liquid into solid fat. Trans fats don't have to be included on food labels, but hydrogenated oils do, so look out for them when shopping. Most supermarkets have now removed trans fats from their products because of health concerns. In reality we consume less than the 5g daily guideline amount of trans fats in the UK, and worries are mainly directed at people who eat a lot of cheap, processed food like pies, biscuits and cake.

The Lowdown on Salt

- High levels of salt in our diet can cause high blood pressure, which is linked in turn to cardiovascular disease.

- The recommended daily intake of salt for an adult is 6g (about a teaspoonful).

- Some food labels give the sodium, rather than salt content. To convert to salt multiply by 2.5.

- 'Reduced salt' products need only contain 25 per cent less salt than the standard product, so if it's very salty in the first place . . .

- Certain foods are obviously high in salt — crisps, salted nuts, food packaged in brine, to name a few. However salt levels in ready-made foods are not so easy to detect. For example, a 400g can of baked beans contains nearly half the daily recommended intake for adults.

The Lowdown on Sugar

- Sugar is a form of carbohydrate, and there are several different types. Some occur naturally in fruit and dairy products, others are added to cakes, sweets and drinks. It's the sugar and sweeteners found in these processed foods that we need to watch because excessive amounts can lead to serious weight gain and all its health-related risks. The higher up the label they are, the more the product contains.

- Food labels can be confusing because they may state only the amount of carbohydrate — even in healthier forms, like wholegrains or pulses — so you can't work out the sugar content. To do this, look out for the phrase 'carbohydrates, of which sugars . . . ' to work out what the balance is.

High or low?

Food labels often display their nutritional information as an amount per 100 grams — not very helpful. The table below sets it out simply — use it to help you choose healthier options:

	High (more than per 100g)	Low (less than per 100g)
Fat	20g	3g
Saturated Fat	5g	1.5g
Salt	1.25g	0.25g
Sugar	15g	5g

Vitamins and Minerals

If you're a healthy adult and you eat a wide range of foods you probably don't need to take health supplements. Vitamin D is the only vitamin we can't get enough of from our diets as it is made mainly by the reaction of our skin to direct sunlight (see Lunchtime, page 88). Fussy eaters, however, and people who exclude certain foods like wheat, dairy or meat and fish may need to supplement their diet to make sure they aren't missing out on essential nutrients.

There are EU official recommended daily allowances (RDAs) for our vitamins and mineral intake, but they vary for pregnant or breastfeeding women, children under six and people over sixty-five, and those with certain medical conditions. They should consult their GP or midwife. There is more information on taking specific supplements in the Breakfast section (pages 37–41) and nhs.uk contains a comprehensive table of the RDA for vitamins and minerals.

Acknowledgements

I have used many websites, books and articles in the course of my research: a full (I hope) list appears over the next few pages. There are several sources to which I have returned repeatedly because I found them so extensive, reliable and clearly written. The Cochrane Collaboration provides helpful overviews of medical studies, and PubMed Health offers access to thousands of research papers. For health information, nhs.uk is an excellent source of official advice and its Behind the Headlines section is a must-read for anyone trying to cut through the hype of some media reports on health research. Professor Richard Wiseman's book *59 Seconds: Think a Little, Change a Lot* is a thorough and readable account of psychological research that is head and shoulders above most self-help books. The British Psychological Society's Research Blog is excellent at summarizing the latest news and developments.

Finally I am indebted to all my colleagues, past and present, on *The Times*'s Body&Soul section, the paper's health and science desks, and particularly to Amanda Ursell. I would also like to thank Professor Anne Murcott for her encouragement and support.

A
David Allen, davidco.com
American Academy of Dermatology
answers.com

B
bbc.co.uk/health
BBC TV
Rosemary Besson
British Heart Foundation
bmjbesthealth.com
British Liver Trust
British Psychological Society Research Blog
British Snoring and Sleep Apnoea Society
British Soft Drinks Association
Burkeman, Oliver, *Help! How to Become Slightly Happier and Get a Bit More Done*, Canongate Books, Edinburgh, 2011
Professor Tanya Byron

C
caloriecount.about.com
caloriesperhour.com
Jane Clarke
Cochrane Collaboration

D

Daily Telegraph
DEFRA
Department of Health
direct.gov.uk

E

Edinburgh and London Sleep Centres
ESA research

F

Food Standards Agency
Professor Russell Foster
Foundation for the Study of Infant Deaths

G

Suzi Godson, moresexdaily.com
Ben Goldacre, badscience.net
Googlescholar
Nina Grunfeld, lifeclubs.co.uk
Guardian

H

Health on the Net Foundation
Health Protection Agency
Professor Jim Horne
howstuffworks.com

L

Lehrer, Jonah, *The Decisive Moment*, Canongate Books, Edinburgh, 2009

Lillenfeld, Scott O. et al., *50 Great Myths of Popular Psychology*, Wiley Blackwell, USA, 2010

livestrong.com

M

Andrew G. Marshall

Mayoclinic.com

Jane McGonigal

Medline Plus

menshealth.co.uk

Professor Anne Murcott

N

netdoctor.co.uk

New Scientist

nhs.uk

NSPCC

P

patient.co.uk

psychologicalscience.org

Psychology Today

Q

quackwatch.com

R

Reader's Digest Association, *5 Minute Health Boosters,*
London, 2010
Matt Roberts
RoSPA

S

Sleep Council
straightstatistics.org

T

The Times

U

UK Society of Chiropodists and Podiatrists
Amanda Ursell

W

webmedmd.boots.com
weightlossresources.co.uk
Wikipedia
Wiseman, Professor Richard, *59 Seconds: Think a Little, Change a Lot*, Macmillan, London, 2009
World Health Organization

Z

Zinczenko, David, with Goulding, Matt, *Eat This, Not That*, Rodale, New York, 2009

We do hope that you have enjoyed reading this large print book.

Did you know that all of our titles are available for purchase?

We publish a wide range of high quality large print books including:
Romances, Mysteries, Classics
General Fiction
Non Fiction and Westerns

Special interest titles available in large print are:
The Little Oxford Dictionary
Music Book
Song Book
Hymn Book
Service Book

Also available from us courtesy of Oxford University Press:
Young Readers' Dictionary
(large print edition)
Young Readers' Thesaurus
(large print edition)

For further information or a free brochure, please contact us at:
Ulverscroft Large Print Books Ltd.,
The Green, Bradgate Road, Anstey,
Leicester, LE7 7FU, England.
Tel: (00 44) 0116 236 4325
Fax: (00 44) 0116 234 0205

THE PUPPY DIARIES

Jill Abramson

'Scout woke every morning at six on the dot. She immediately started crying . . . but she always cheered up the minute she had company . . . The soulful brown eyes that greeted me had long lashes that gave Scout a sultry, flirtatious look; she was a canine version of Veronica Lake . . . ' What happens when a smart New York Times editor decides to fill her empty nest with a puppy? This is the marvellously entertaining (and instructive) chronicle of an adorable golden retriever puppy named Scout. Part memoir, part manual, The Puppy Diaries recounts Jill Abramson's experiences of the first year of puppy parenting.

LONG LOST FAMILY

Humphrey Price

Mothers reunited with their sons and daughters; children finally meeting their fathers; siblings brought together for the first time — *Long Lost Family* tells the stories of families brought together after years apart. There's Jennifer, who knew she had a twin sister, but had never seen her — unaware that she lived just a few miles away. Then there's Karen, who discovered her older sister was actually her birth mother, and her search for the father she'd never known. This companion to ITV's TV show reveals the determination to fill the gap in people's lives caused by a decision taken years before . . .